327 World Bank Discussion Papers

Agricultural Reform in Russia

A View from the Farm Level

Karen Brooks
Elmira Krylatykh
Zvi Lerman
Aleksandr Petrikov
Vasilii Uzun

Recent World Bank Discussion Papers

No. 257   *Improving the Quality of Primary Education in Latin America: Towards the 21st Century.* Lawrence Wolff, Ernesto Schiefelbein, and Jorge Valenzuela

No. 258   *How Fast is Fertility Declining in Botswana and Zimbabwe?* Duncan Thomas and Ityai Muvandi

No. 259   *Policies Affecting Fertility and Contraceptive Use: An Assessment of Twelve Sub-Saharan Countries.* Susan Scribner

No. 260   *Financial Systems in Sub-Saharan Africa: A Comparative Study.* Paul A. Popiel

No. 261   *Poverty Alleviation and Social Investment Funds: The Latin American Experience.* Philip J. Glaessner, Kye Woo Lee, Anna Maria Sant'Anna, and Jean-Jacques de St. Antoine

No. 262   *Public Policy for the Promotion of Family Farms in Italy: The Experience of the Fund for the Formation of Peasant Property.* Eric B. Shearer and Giuseppe Barbero

No. 263   *Self-Employment for the Unemployed: Experience in OECD and Transitional Economies.* Sandra Wilsonand Arvil V. Adams

No. 264   *Schooling and Cognitive Achievements of Children in Morocco: Can the Government Improve Outcomes?* Shahidur R. Khandker, Victor Lavy, and Deon Filmer

No. 265   *World BankÄFinanced Projects with Community Participation: Procurement and Disbursement Issues.* Gita Gopal and Alexandre Marc

No. 266   *Seed Systems in Sub-Saharan Africa: Issues and Options.* V. Venkatesan

No. 267   *Trade Policy Reform in Developing Countries since 1985: A Review of the Evidence.* Judith M. Dean, Seema Desai, and James Riedel

No. 268   *Farm Restructuring and Land Tenure in Reforming Socialist Economies: A Comparative Analysis of Eastern and Central Europe.* Euroconsult and Centre for World Food Studies

No. 269   *The Evolution of the World Bank's Railway Lending.* Alice Galenson and Louis S. Thompson

No. 270   *Land Reform and Farm Restructuring in Ukraine.* Zvi Lerman, Karer. Brooks, and Csaba Csaki

No. 271   *Small Enterprises Adjusting to Liberalization in Five African Countries.* Ron Parker, Randall Riopelle, and William F. Steel

No. 272   *Adolescent Health: Reassessing the Passage to Adulthood.* Judith Senderowitz

No. 273   *Measurement of Welfare Changes Caused by Large Price Shifts: An Issue in the Power Sector.* Robert Bacon

No. 274   *Social Action Programs and Social Funds: A Review of Design and Implementation in Sub-Saharan Africa.* Alexandre Marc, Carol Graham, Mark Schacter, and Mary Schmidt

No. 275   *Investing in Young Children.* Mary Eming Young

No. 276   *Managing Primary Health Care: Implications of the Health Transition.* Richard Heaver

No. 277   *Energy Demand in Five Major Asian Developing Countries: Structure and Prospects.* Masayasu Ishiguro and Takamasa Akiyama

No. 278   *Preshipment Inspection Services.* Patrick Low

No. 279   *Restructuring Banks and Enterprises: Recent Lessons from Transition Countries.* Michael S. Borish, Millard F. Long, and Michel Noël

No. 280   *Agriculture, Poverty, and Policy Reform in Sub-Saharan Africa.* Kevin M. Cleaver and W. Graeme Donovan

No. 281   *The Diffusion of Information Technology: Experience of Industrial Countries and Lessons for Developing Countries.* Nagy Hanna, Ken Guy, and Erik Arnold

No. 282   *Trade Laws and Institutions: Good Practices and the World Trade Organization.* Bernard M. Hoekman

No. 283   *Meeting the Challenge of Chinese Enterprise Reform.* Harry G. Broadman

No. 284   *Desert Locust Management: A Time for Change.* Steen R. Joffe

No. 285   *Sharing the Wealth: Privatization through Broad-based Ownership Strategies.* Stuart W. Bell

No. 286   *Credit Policies and the Industrialization of Korea.* Yoon Je Cho and Joon-Kyung Kim

No. 287   *East Asia's Environment: Principles and Priorities for Action.* Jeffrey S. Hammer and Sudhir Shetty

No. 288   *Africa's Experience with Structural Adjustment: Proceedings of the Harare Seminar, May 23-24, 1994.* Edited by Kapil Kapoor

No. 289   *Rethinking Research on Land Degradation in Developing Countries.* Yvan Biot, Piers Macleod Blaikie, Cecile Jackson, and Richard Palmer-Jones

No. 290   *Decentralizing Infrastructure: Advantages and Limitations.* Edited by Antonio Estache

(Continued on the inside back cover)

327 🌐 World Bank Discussion Papers

Agricultural Reform in Russia

A View from the Farm Level

Karen Brooks
Elmira Krylatykh
Zvi Lerman
Aleksandr Petrikov
Vasilii Uzun

The World Bank
Washington, D.C.

Discussion Papers present results of country analysis or research that are circulated to encourage discussion and comment within the development community. To present these results with the least possible delay, the typescript of this paper has not been prepared in accordance with the procedures appropriate to formal printed texts, and the World Bank accepts no responsibility for errors. Some sources cited in this paper may be informal documents that are not readily available.

The findings, interpretations, and conclusions expressed in this paper are entirely those of the author(s) and should not be attributed in any manner to the World Bank, to its affiliated organizations, or to members of its Board of Executive Directors or the countries they represent. The World Bank does not guarantee the accuracy of the data included in this publication and accepts no responsibility whatsoever for any consequence of their use. The boundaries, colors, denominations, and other information shown on any map in this volume do not imply on the part of the World Bank Group any judgment on the legal status of any territory or the endorsement or acceptance of such boundaries.

The material in this publication is copyrighted. Requests for permission to reproduce portions of it should be sent to the Office of the Publisher at the address shown in the copyright notice above. The World Bank encourages dissemination of its work and will normally give permission promptly and, when the reproduction is for noncommercial purposes, without asking a fee. Permission to copy portions for classroom use is granted through the Copyright Clearance Center, Inc., Suite 910, 222 Rosewood Drive, Danvers, Massachusetts 01923, U.S.A.

The complete backlist of publications from the World Bank is shown in the annual Index of Publications, which contains an alphabetical title list (with full ordering information) and indexes of subjects, authors, and countries and regions. The latest edition is available free of charge from the Distribution Unit, Office of the Publisher, The World Bank, 1818 H Street, N.W., Washington, D.C. 20433, U.S.A., or from Publications, The World Bank, 66, avenue d'Iéna, 75116 Paris, France.

ISSN: 0259-210X

Karen Brooks is principal economist in the Sector Policy and Water Resources Division of the World Bank's Agriculture and Natural Resources Department. Elmira Krylatykh is a senior researcher at the Agrarian Institute, Moscow, Russian Federation. Zvi Lerman is a senior lecturer, Department of Agricultural Economics and Management, the Hebrew University, Rehovot, Israel. Aleksandr Petrikov is director of, and Vasilii Uzun is a senior researcher at, the Agrarian Institute, Moscow.

Library of Congress Cataloging-in-Publication Data

Agricultural reform in Russia : a view from the farm level / Karen
Brooks ... [et al.].
    p.   cm. — (World Bank discussion papers ; 327)
  Includes bibliographical references.
  ISBN 0-8213-3655-X
  1. Agriculture—Economic aspects—Russia (Federation).
2. Agriculture and state—Russia (Federation). 3. Russia—
(Federation)—Rural conditions. 4. Agricultural laws and
legislation—Russia (Federation). 5. Agriculture—Economic aspects—
Russia (Federation)—Statistics. 6. Agriculture and state—Russia
(Federation)—Statistics. 7. Russia (Federation)—Rural conditions—
Statistics   I. Brooks, Karen McConnell.
HD1995.15.A65   1996
338.1'847—dc20
                                              96-20414
                                              CIP

Contents

FOREWORD ix

ABSTRACT xi

INTRODUCTION xiii
    The Composition and Geography of the Sample xiii
    Scientific and Technical Team xv
    References xvi

SUMMARY AND CONCLUSIONS xvii

1. RUSSIAN AGRICULTURE: 1992-1994 1
    Recent Changes in Land Tenure and Farm Organization 1
    Sectoral Performance During the Period 1991-1994 3
    Profitability and Incentives 4
    Farm Finances, Debt, and Investment 7
    Marketing of Output 9
    Agricultural Trade 10
    List of Data Sources in Chapter 1 13

2. THE LEGAL FRAMEWORK FOR LAND MARKETS AND REORGANIZATION OF FARMS 15
    Russian Land Law 15
        Land Ownership 16
        Land Transactions 18
        Mortgage of Land 20
    Farm Restructuring 20
    The Ambiguous Status of Land Shares 22
        Treatment of Land Shares in Government Resolution No. 96 22
        Treatment of Land Shares in Recent Legislation 23
        Treatment of Land Shares in Draft Land Code 24
    Outcomes and Next Steps 24
        Size Distribution of Reorganized Russian Farms 25
        Exit: The Need for a Mechanism 26
    References to Chapter 2 27

3. REORGANIZATION OF LARGE FARM ENTERPRISES 29
    Exits of Employees During Reorganization 32
    Attitudes toward Ownership of Land 33
    Organization and Changes in Farm Management 34
    Production in Farm Enterprises 35
        Crops 35
        Livestock 36
    Labor 37
    Farm Inputs and Services 38
    Marketing 41
    Processing 43
    Social Services and Benefits 44
    Perceived Difficulties During Reorganization 45
    Finance and Credit 45

4. FARM EMPLOYEES 49
    Demographic Profile 49
    Employees and Farm Reorganization 50
    Family Income 51
    Plot Structure and Tenure 52
    Attitude Toward Private Farming 54
    Household Production: Livestock and Crops 54
    Marketing 55
    Social Services and Expectations 57

5. PRIVATE FARMERS 59
    Demographic Profile 59
    Farm Size and Ownership 60
    Attitude toward Ownership of Land 63
    Family Income 63
    Production 64
    Labor and Machinery 66
    Marketing 67
    Farm Inputs 69
    Cooperation 71
    Debt and Finances 72

List of Tables

A.	General Characteristics of the Five Sampled Provinces	xiv
B.	Distribution of Respondents by Provinces in Two Surveys	xv
1.1.	Land Holding by Type of User in Russia: 1991-1995	1
1.2.	Share of Land and Production by Farm Category in 1994	1
1.3.	Agricultural Enterprises of Different Organizational Forms	2
1.4.	Share of Agriculture in GDP and Index of Gross Agricultural Output in Russia: 1990-1994	3
1.5.	Livestock Numbers and Sectoral Structure of the Herd in Russia	5
1.6.	Index of Gross Agricultural Output in Economies in Transition	5
1.7.	Index Numbers of Prices for Agricultural Outputs and Inputs in Russia	6
1.8.	Domestic and Border Prices in Russia: 1993-1994	6
1.9.	Index of Investment in Russia: 1990-1994	8
1.10.	Financial Position of Russian Agriculture	8
1.11.	Working Capital Position of Russian Agriculture	8
1.12.	Change in Marketing Channels in Russia: 1991-1994	10
1.13.	Prices in Various Marketing Channels in Russia: Third Quarter 1994	11
1.14.	Russian Imports: 1990-1994	11
1.15.	Food Imports to Russia from Non-FSU Countries	11
2.1.	Forms of Land Tenure and Associated Disposition Rights in the Russian Civil Code	17
2.2.	Nizhnii Novgorod Farm Restructuring Procedure	21
3.1.	Forms of Farm Reorganization	29
3.2.	Rights Associated with Land and Asset Shares:	31
3.3.	Exit of Employees During Reorganization of Farm Enterprises	33
3.4.	Expected Changes as a Result of Farm-Enterprise Reorganization	34
3.5.	Production and Product Mix in Russian Farm Enterprises 1990-1994	35
3.6.	Structure of Production and Sales	35
3.7.	Crop Production and Structure of Planted Area in Farm Enterprises: 1992-1993	36
3.8.	Livestock Production in Farm Enterprises	37
3.9.	Number of Animals per Farm and per Producer	37
3.10.	Labor Resources in Russian Farm Enterprises: 1990-1993	37
3.11.	Wages in Russian Farm Enterprises, October 1993	37
3.12.	Management Strategies: What to Do If No Money to Meet Payroll?	38
3.13.	Access to Different Supply Channels for Farm Inputs and Services	39
3.14.	Enterprises Acting as Suppliers of Farm Inputs	40
3.15.	Cooperation in Purchase and Use of Inputs	40
3.16.	Reported Difficulties in Purchase of Farm Inputs	41
3.17.	Services Supplied by Farm Enterprises to Rural Residents	41
3.18.	Proportion of Output Consumed and Sold by Producers	42
3.19.	Main Marketing Channel by Commodity	42
3.20.	Marketing Problems as Reported by Farm-Enterprise Managers	43
3.21.	Processing Facilities in Farm Enterprises	43
3.22.	Payment in Kind to Farms from Processors	43
3.23.	Transfer of Social Assets to Local Council	44
3.24.	Perceived Difficulties During Reorganization	45
3.25.	"What to Do with Farm Debt During Reorganization?"	46
3.26.	Loan Collateral Used by Farm Managers: 1992-1994	46
3.27.	"What Farm Structures will Have the Greatest Difficulty Obtaining Credit Next Year?"	47
3.28.	Anticipated Access to Credit for Private Farmers Compared to Collectives	47

4.1.	Ownership of Housing in Employee Families	49
4.2.	Education Profile of Employee Families	50
4.3.	Occupation Profile of Employee Families	50
4.4.	Salary Delays in Farm Enterprises, 1992-1993	51
4.5.	Supplementary Income in Kind Paid to Employees in 1993	52
4.6.	Household Plots as Reported by Russian Managers and Employees	52
4.7.	Land Tenure and Sources of Land in Household Plots	53
4.8.	Average Size and Composition of a Household Plot	53
4.9.	Views of Private Farming Expressed by Members and Employees of Farm Enterprises	54
4.10.	Production in Household Plots	55
4.11.	Livestock in Households	55
4.12.	Employees Reporting Production and Commercial Sales by Product	56
4.13.	Marketing Channels for Household Plots	56
4.14.	Prices Received by Households and Farm Enterprises	57
4.15.	Reported Availability of Social Services and Benefits	58
5.1.	Education Profile of Private Farmers and Farm Employees	59
5.2.	Housing of Private Farmers	60
5.3.	Average Size of Private Farms and Structure of Land Use	61
5.4.	Distribution of Number of Households per Private Farm	61
5.5.	Average Size of Single-Family and Multi-Family Farms	62
5.6.	Structure of Land Tenure in Private Farms	62
5.7.	Sources of Land in Private Farms by Province	63
5.8.	Preferred Form of Land Tenure in Private Farms and Household Plots	63
5.9.	Attitude to Buy-and-Sell Transactions in Land	63
5.10.	Employment of Head of Household and Spouse in Private-Farmer Families	64
5.11.	Production of Private Farms and Household Plots	65
5.12.	Livestock in Private Farms and Household Plots	66
5.13.	Farm Labor and Farm Size Indicators	67
5.14.	Farmers with Agricultural Machinery	67
5.15.	Proportion of Output Consumed and Sold by Private Farmers	67
5.16.	Main Marketing Channels by Commodity	68
5.17.	Marketing Problems as Reported by Private Farmers	69
5.18.	Prices Received by Farm Enterprises, Households, and Private Farmers	69
5.19.	Use of Different Supply Channels for Farm Inputs and Services	70
5.20.	Reported Difficulties with Purchase of Farm Inputs and Services	71
5.21.	Cooperation Among Private Farmers 1992-1994	71
5.22.	Farmers Owning "Less than a Whole Machine"	71
5.23.	Collateral Used by Private Farmers: 1992-1994	72
5.24.	Growth of Assets and Sales in Private Farms	73
5.25.	Sources of Annual Investment Flows	74
5.26.	Cost-to-Sales Ratio in Russian Farms: 1990-1993	74

List of Figures

1.1. Changes in Product Mix in Russia: 1990-1994 2
1.2. Livestock in Russia 4
1.3. Average Payment and Collection Period 9
1.4. Wages by Economic Sector in Russia 10
2.1. Size Distribution of Farm Enterprises: Russia 1990-1993 25
2.2   Size Distribution of New Farms: Orel, Rostov, Ryazan Provinces 26
2.3. Size Distribution of New Farms: Nizhnii Novgorod Province 26
2.4. Size Distribution of US Farms 26
3.1. Size Distribution of Farm Enterprises: 1990-1993 30
3.2. Land Ownership in Farm Enterprises 30
3.3. Exit of Employees During Reorganization 33
3.4. Proportion of Farm Wages in Total Expenditure 38
3.5. Provision of Social Services and Benefits: 1992-1994 44
3.6. Accounts Receivable of Farm Enterprises 47
4.1. Age Distribution in Employee Households 49
4.2. How Has the Family Situation Changed? 57
4.3. What the Family Budget Buys 57
4.4. Perception of Family Future 57
5.1. Size Distribution of Private Farms 60
5.2. Land Tenure in Private Farms 62
5.3. Farm Income: Private Farmers and Employees 64
5.4. Product Mix in Different Farm Categories 65
5.5. Number of Employed in Private Farms 66
5.6. Sources of Investment Funds 74

Foreword

Russia's agricultural sector has potential to make a significant contribution to global food supply in the coming century. The country's agriculture is now, however, under-performing. Production continues to decline and productivity is low. At a time when world grain stocks are at historic lows, Russia is a net importer of grain despite the country's clear potential to become a major exporter. Poor performance of the agricultural sector has eroded the well-being of Russia's rural people, and impedes resumption of aggregate growth.

The reasons for continued decline are complex and only partially understood. Land tenure relations and farm organization are among the most important issues that must be better understood if new approaches to sectoral recovery are to be crafted. The present study attempts to clarify these issues by examining the situation in Russian agriculture at the farm level after four years of reforms.

The primary purpose of this joint study by experts from Russia and the World Bank is to enrich the information base for consideration of policy. In Russia, as in all market economies, policy makers can make informed decisions only if they have access to information and empirical analysis. The study does not offer explicit policy recommendations, but instead indicates areas of high priority for additional analytical work. One conclusion of the study is that the process of structural change in Russian agriculture is far from complete. The legal environment should therefore protect mechanisms for continued restructuring, and not lock in place a structure created at the earliest stage of reform. Analysts should continue to clarify the factors affecting performance of the sector, and shaping its structural evolution. They should continue to document the impact of measures adopted to date.

Policy debates in democratic societies reflect a wide range of views, and many factors affect measures adopted. The quality of information available during debate can at times make a significant contribution toward consensus to move ahead. The World Bank supports the work presented in this study as part of its on-going efforts to assist the Government of Russia, and indeed the governments of all countries in the former Soviet Union, in improving the well-being of rural people.

Alexander McCalla
Director
Agriculture and Natural Resources Department
The World Bank

Abstract

Russia has had a formal program of land reform and farm restructuring in place since 1991. Land and asset shares have been distributed to most farm workers, but the legal status of these shares remains ambiguous, and the practical mechanisms for exit of individuals and restructuring of the large farm enterprises are mostly undecided. After four years of formal reforms, the traditional agricultural enterprises are still largely intact, and functioning much as they did in the past, although with poorer economic outcomes. Farm enterprises have diminished in size, but remain very large compared to farms in market economies.

The ongoing reforms have produced a radical change in the distribution of land ownership in Russia. As of 1994, the state holds less than 20% of agricultural land, while the individual private sector, including the augmented subsidiary household plots and around 200,000 private farmers, accounts for 12% of farmland. The remaining 70% of agricultural land is in collective management, most of it divided into paper shares to individuals.

Few shareholders express intentions to exit from the enterprises and use their land and asset shares to establish independent private farms. The main reasons cited by respondents in the survey are insufficiency of capital for start-up, difficulty affording needed farm inputs, and unwillingness to assume the risks involved. Farm employees express intention to remain within their enterprises, but they are markedly more pessimistic than private farmers about the outlook for their families' economic futures.

Low prices for agricultural products adversely affect the ability of farms to generate earnings, and combine with poorly developed financial services to constrain agricultural recovery. The role of land markets in providing liquidity for farm enterprises is poorly understood, and the legal framework for land transactions is ambiguous and contested. Markets for commercial agricultural land function in a restricted way, as use rights are allocated and reallocated and farm enterprises and individuals lease land in and out. Enterprise managers and employees see little positive role for market transactions in land. Private farmers are more supportive of fully functioning land markets, but even among this group only a slim majority supports rights to purchase and sell agricultural land.

Rural social services are deteriorating. Farm managers are cutting back on expenditures for social services, and there has been relatively little transfer of social assets to local governments. Most local governments have no budget to accept the financial and administrative responsibilities for social services.

Russia's agricultural reforms have initiated important changes, but have not yet arrested the decline in sectoral performance and rural well-being. Accelerated development of land markets and other institutions that can deliver better marketing and financial services to agricultural producers, and thus increase farm earnings and rural savings, will be key to recovery and growth.

Introduction

The changes in Russian agriculture that began at the end of 1991 with the dissolution of the Soviet Union are usually represented by aggregate statistical data. In addition to the overall picture of agricultural reforms presented by these official statistics, it is interesting and instructive to examine the process of reform on the micro level in order to understand the impact on existing farms and individuals in rural communities. Such micro-level monitoring of reforms in Russian agriculture was undertaken in two extensive field surveys conducted by the Agrarian Institute of the Russian Academy of Agricultural Sciences with the participation and support of the World Bank. The first survey was carried out between October 1992 and March 1993. The detailed findings have been published in Brooks and Lerman (1994), and a condensed Russian version in Brooks, Krylatykh, Lerman, and Uzun (1994). The second survey was conducted a year later, between November 1993 and April 1994, and the following chapters provide an analysis and a summary of the recent findings.

Both surveys addressed three groups of active rural agents: managers of large-scale farm enterprises (the traditional collective and state farms), which started to reorganize at the end of 1991 and still account for the bulk of agricultural production in Russia; members and employees of these enterprises as typical representatives of the rural population in Russia; and the emerging private farmers, who began to establish family farms outside the collectivist framework in 1991-1992. The two surveys largely used the same questionnaires. The first survey was based on 2700 interviews, and the second on 1800. Both surveys were conducted in the same geographical area, but the specific respondents differed because not all individual participants in the first sample could be located, and because the numbers of farm units changed through ongoing reorganization. The two samples overlap, but are not identical.

The monograph starts with a summary chapter that presents the main conclusions of the study. The summary is followed by two general chapters that analyze the economic context of the reforms in Russian agriculture (Chapter 1) and provide a summary of the current legal framework (Chapter 2). The introductory material is followed by three chapters that present the detailed findings of the second survey conducted between November 1993 and April 1994. The presentation of the findings is organized around the three main groups of respondents: reorganization of large farm enterprises as reported by managers (Chapter 3), the participation of farm-enterprise employees in the process of reform (Chapter 4), and the situation of private farmers (Chapter 5). The main topics covered in each chapter include land use and tenure during reform, production and labor in a changing environment, adjustment of marketing and supply channels to new conditions, farm finances, and changes in provision of and access to social services in the process of reorganization.

The survey data in Chapters 3-5 reflect developments at the farm level up to early 1994. However, the aggregate data to January 1995 used in Chapters 1 and 2 suggest relatively little change in farm organization and land tenure since the completion of the survey. The study thus can be used to judge the progress of Russian agricultural reforms through 1994.

Throughout the monograph, tables and figures presented without an explicitly identified source are based on survey data. The data of the first survey are identified as 1992, while 1994 identifies the data of the second survey. Data collected in the 1994 survey often refer to 1993 performance (e.g., production, labor, or borrowing). Publications presenting the results of the first survey are listed at the end of the Introduction. Brief lists of relevant references are given at the end of Chapters 1 and 2. Chapters 3-5 in their entirety are based on the data of the second survey (1994), with comparisons to the first survey (1992).

The Composition and Geography of the Sample

The pace and course of reform varies geographically, depending in part on agroclimatic factors, and in part on policies determined at the province and district levels. In order to clarify restructuring at the farm level and take into account regional variation, five provinces (*oblasts*) were included in the sample. Pskov, Orel, Rostov, Saratov, and Novosibirsk provinces were chosen to capture a range of agroclimatic conditions and farm specialization profiles. Four of the five provinces are located in the European part of Russia, and Novosibirsk Province is in Siberia. The general characteristics of the provinces are presented in Table A. The local research organizations in these provinces were sufficiently experienced and qualified to carry out the field work.

Table A. General Characteristics of the Five Sampled Provinces

	Saratov	*Rostov*	*Novosibirsk*	*Orel*	*Pskov*
Location	Lower Volga Region, SE part of Eastern European Plain	North-Caucasus Region, Don basin, S of East European Plain	SE of West Siberian Plain, between Ob' and Irtysh rivers	Central Russian plateau, center part	NW European Russia, border with Belarus, Latvia, Estonia
Farm land	8.4 M ha	8.5 M ha	8 M ha	1.9 M ha	1.6 M ha
Precipitation	275-360 mm (left bank) 400-460 mm (right bank)	400-650 mm	300-450 mm		550-650 mm
Climate	Dry continental, droughts, winds	Moderate continental, hot and dry	Extreme continental, short hot summer, drought & winds in the south	Moderate continental, warm, moderately humid	Moderate continental
Soils	Heavy: 50% chernozem, 30% chestnut, 11% solonetz	Chernozem, chestnut, solonetz	Podzol, serozem, chernozem	Chernozem, serozem, dernopodzol, sandy	Podzolic, marshy
Agriculture	Russia's main grain producer, livestock, large farms	Russia's main livestock producer, mechanized mixed farming	Mixed grain-livestock	Diversified crops, grain-livestock farms	Mixed dairy-beef, flax
Remarks	Inclusion of irrigated land in farm restructuring presents special issues	Variety of farm enterprise structures		Intensive use of farm land: 87.3% plowed, only 9.1% forested	Family farms near border with Latvia, Estonia; leader in private farm registration; 30% forested

Farm-enterprise managers and employees were surveyed in a total of 14 districts (*rayons*) selected among the five provinces: three districts from each of Novosibirsk, Orel, and Rostov provinces, four districts from Saratov Province, and one district from Pskov Province. Survey instruments were administered to managers of most farm enterprises in the selected districts. In this way, enterprises of different organizational forms and past history of profitability were chosen. The sample of households was drawn from a subset of the selected enterprises. Farmers were surveyed in 18 districts, which included the same 14 districts selected for managers and employees plus four additional districts in Novosibirsk Province. The number of districts had to be increased in order to achieve a sample with the required number of private farmers. The sample was chosen at random from the list of all registered farmers in each district, giving preference to geographically clustered farms to save travel time for the enumerators. The respondents consisted of 234 farm-enterprise managers, 507 farm-enterprise employees, and 1030 private farmers. In total, 1771 interviews were conducted. The composition of the 1994 sample is shown in Table B, which gives for comparison also the composition of the sample from the first survey (1992). Although the 1994 sample was substantially smaller than the 1992 sample (1771 interviews in 1993 compared to 2671 in 1992), the reduction mainly involved fewer interviews with farm-enterprise employees, while the number of interviews with farm managers and private farmers was practically the same in both surveys (Table B).

Table B. Distribution of Respondents by Provinces in Two Surveys

Province	1994 Survey			1992 Survey		
	Farm Managers	Farm Employees	Private Farmers	Farm Managers	Farm Employees	Private Farmers
Saratov	61	144	273	101	403	324
Rostov	51	110	200	35	306	293
Novosibirsk	58	110	250	43	300	142
Orel	52	113	177	70	318	125
Pskov	12	30	130	11	100	100
TOTAL	**234**	**507**	**1030**	**260**	**1427**	**984**

Scientific and Technical Team

The study was the result of a cooperative effort of teams of researchers from the Agrarian Institute in Moscow and the World Bank. Elmira Krylatykh, Vasilii Uzun, and Aleksander Petrikov led the work of the Agrarian Institute and prepared a Russian draft of the report, providing valuable input on Russian legislation and the overall status of reform in the country. The were assisted by N. Shagaida, R. Yanbykh, M. Kuznetsov, T. Yakovleva, N. Lebedeva, Z. Chibisova, and E. Kunina. On behalf of the World Bank, Karen Brooks and Zvi Lerman participated in the design of the study and undertook the analysis of the survey data. They also wrote the English version of the present monograph. Valuable technical support was provided in Moscow by Vyacheslav Mironov, Andrei Gorbal', and Aleksander Zhitkin, and in Washington by Apparao Katikineni.

The two surveys were conducted with the support and encouragement of the late Academician Aleksander Nikonov, then Director of the Agrarian Institute. We dedicate this monograph to his memory.

References

K. Brooks and Z. Lerman. 1993. "Land Reform and Farm Restructuring in Russia: 1992 Status," *American Journal of Agricultural Economics*, Vol. 75, pp. 1254-1259, December.

K. Brooks and Z. Lerman. 1994. *Land Reform and Farm Restructuring in Russia*, World Bank Discussion Paper 233, The World Bank, Washington, D.C.

K. Brooks, E. Krylatykh, Z. Lerman, and V. Uzun. 1994. "Agrarian Reform and Reorganization of Agricultural Enterprises in Russia," [in Russian], *Agrarian Science*, pp. 6-12, April.

K. Brooks and Z. Lerman. 1995a. "Restructuring of Socialized Farms and New Land Relations in Russia," in: D. Umali-Deininger and C. Maguire, eds., *Agriculture in Liberalizing Economies: Changing Roles for Governments*, The World Bank, Washington, D.C., pp. 145-172.

K. Brooks and Z. Lerman. 1995b. "Restructuring of Traditional Farms and New Land Relations in Russia," *Agricultural Economics*, Vol. 13, pp. 11-25.

Summary and Conclusions

Russian agricultural output declined in 1995 for the fifth consecutive year. Agricultural workers are reported to earn one third of the average Russian wage, but few leave agriculture for better alternatives. Investment in agriculture has declined markedly, and producers have cut back on use of purchased inputs that enhance yields and preserve soil fertility. The well-being of Russia's 40 million rural people has declined through processes that many do not understand, and pessimism and resignation are wide-spread.

The reduction in agricultural output in Russia is consistent with the experience in many countries in transition. In fact, the decline in Russia is not as severe as in other countries in the former Soviet Union and in Eastern and Central Europe. Moreover, a reduction in gross product can be part of a process of adjustment as the sector orients toward new markets, new products, and new production technologies. For example, Hungary's decline in gross agricultural output of approximately one third during the transitional period has been accompanied by profound changes in economic policy and institutions, and modest growth has now resumed on a more competitive and dynamic basis. In Russia, the changes in policy and institutions have also been significant, but not sufficient to reverse or even arrest the deterioration in sectoral performance. Russian leaders now face the task of determining why the deterioration continues and what can be done about it.

The policy debate in Russia is dominated by two opposing views. Many within the agricultural lobby argue that the government has reduced support for the sector too much, and has moved too quickly with radical reforms. Reformers outside the agricultural lobby and often outside the sector argue that budgetary support for agriculture is still excessive and reforms are too slow. Between the extreme positions of "too much reform, too little support" and "too much support, too little reform" there is little common ground. Moreover, the two positions imply quite different policy prescriptions.

When democratic societies are divided by fundamental disagreement on important matters of policy, the issues are aired in public debate informed by research and empirical analysis. In Russia, the public debate has been characterized largely by assertions and pronouncements, often unsupported by empirical evidence. Basic indicators of the magnitude of government support or net taxation, and the identification of instruments of delivery are missing in the policy debate. Assertions are made about the impact of trade on domestic producers and the need for protection, but the agricultural trade data showing imports and exports consolidated for all trading partners are not readily available, nor included in the discussion. The impact of farm reorganization on sectoral performance is debated without adequate assessment of the extent of reorganization at the farm level. As policy makers turn anew to the difficult problems of Russian agriculture, they will need to draw on solid and current analysis of the state of the sector and the factors that affect its performance.

This study and the two surveys on which it is based are intended as a modest contribution to the empirical base for discussion of agricultural policy in Russia. The surveys conducted in the winter of 1992/93 and the winter of 1993/94 on a large and varied sample of farm enterprises and private farms were designed to provide information on changes in farm organization, ownership of assets, economic behavior, and decision making at the farm level. The surveys suggest several conclusions that should inform discussions of agricultural policy.

Most farms (95%) have complied formally with the decrees mandating reorganization and divestiture of state-owned land. As a consequence of this process, the state now holds relatively little agricultural land (18% in early 1994, compared to full state ownership prior to the reforms). Most farms have registered as closed shareholding organizations, and hold land in collective or cooperative management. The privatization of land and reorganization of enterprises has thus resulted in a strengthening of collective and cooperative production and ownership, and has led to a reduction in the share of state farms and the proportion of state owned land. Approximately 12% of land is now in the individual sector, of which 5% is in private farms and about 3% in household plots.

Most shareholding farms are managed internally like collective farms of the past, but with more administrative autonomy and less financial security than in the past. Farm size in the sample has declined by about 15%, but the farms are still very large, averaging 8000 ha per farm. The labor force has declined less than farm size, and farms have made some adjustment in the production profile, increasing crop production and reducing the relative importance of livestock. Area allotted to household plots has increased (from about one quarter hectare in 1990 to one third at present), but the plot remains subsidiary and retains its traditional relationship with the larger enterprise. Although virtually all farms in the sample have formally reorganized, the change in legal status has brought relatively little change in internal structure and decision making.

Shareholders are aware of their theoretical rights, but perceive little tangible benefit to share ownership. Land and asset shares are at present blended into the asset base of the enterprise. Few farms pay shareholders for land use or dividends on the asset shares, since payroll takes higher priority, and farms have difficulty meeting wage obligations. Since the shares have no perceived value, shareholders see little difference between reorganized enterprises and their predecessors.

Few shareholders express intentions to exit from the enterprises, taking their land and asset shares to establish private farms. Shares would acquire value if holders could withdraw them in real assets, but few farm employees express intention at present to establish independent private farms. Employees cited a number of reasons why they do not intend to enter private farming. Foremost among these were insufficiency of capital for start-up, difficulty affording needed farm inputs, and unwillingness to assume the risks involved. Farm employees expressed intention to remain within their enterprises, but they were markedly more pessimistic than private farmers about the outlook for their families' economic futures. The decision to stay is thus not a reflection of confidence that shareholding farms will be viable enterprises in the future.

If shareholders decide in the future to exit with land and assets, their legal right to do so is ambiguous. During a period of change in farm structure, a natural tension arises between stability of the existing enterprises and dynamism in the form and size of enterprises. A degree of stability is desirable so that new enterprises have a chance to test their viability before undergoing further changes. On the other hand, too much stability locks in place a structure that may not have been optimal at the outset, or may have become "less optimal" over time. The earliest laws and decrees on land reform and farm restructuring recognized the rights of individuals to exit with assets, and did not address the need of enterprises for a degree of stability or at least a mechanism for orderly change. Although few shareholders have chosen to exit, concern about enterprise stability became paramount in 1994 and 1995, and several pieces of existing and pending legislation circumscribe the rights of individuals to withdraw real assets. The pendulum has thus swung greatly to the side of the existing enterprises.

The rights of individuals to exit are not in question; at issue is the right of the enterprise or the individual shareholder to decide on the disposition of property. The present trend in Russian legislative debate is to deny individuals the right to withdraw property, except under restrictive conditions. This trend would lead to corporatization of the existing farm enterprises. There is a strongly held view in Russia that large corporate farms are more efficient and competitive than small or mid-sized farms, and that the large enterprises should be protected from subdivision. This assertion has not been confronted with empirical evidence on farm size and efficiency from around the world. A careful review of the international evidence on farm size and its relation to efficiency would likely raise questions about the wisdom of corporatizing the existing large farm enterprises, and would improve the quality of the debate about the draft Land Code, the draft Law of Cooperatives, and other laws and policies critical to agricultural reform.

Markets for commercial agricultural land do not function now, and enterprise managers and employees see little positive role for market transactions in land. Private farmers were more supportive of fully functioning land markets, but even among this group a slim majority (53%) supported rights to purchase and sell agricultural land. All three groups of respondents supported purchase and sale of household plots and garden plots, but transactions in commercial agricultural land are viewed very differently from transactions in subsidiary plots. Land markets nevertheless function in a constrained way; use rights are allocated and reallocated and farm enterprises lease land in and out. However, open and competitive land markets, in which land values can be observed and on which owners can recoup investments in land improvement and protection, are not functioning at present. Moreover, there is no apparent rural constituency calling for their creation. Even though farm managers and private farmers decried the lack of financing for investment in agriculture and for working capital, the role of land markets in providing liquidity for farm enterprises is poorly understood. Land markets are instead viewed almost exclusively as an arena in which wealth is transferred from producers to speculators.

Producer prices in 1993 and 1994 were below world trading prices by a substantial margin, 30%-40% lower for major commodities such as grain and meat. Prices for inputs were also low, although closer to world prices than were product prices. Low and declining yields, low prices, and a roughly static labor force combine to produce an increase in the share of gross farm earnings paid to labor, despite a substantial fall in real wages. Under current prices and efficiency, enterprises do not generate enough earnings for investment. Nor are they able to borrow at commercial rates, since they lack both collateral and repayment capacity. The farms are thus caught in a cycle of falling earnings and declining efficiency, from which they cannot escape under current prices. Private farmers do not have the same high labor costs and do not carry large numbers of loss-making livestock. Their financial returns are thus somewhat better than is

the case for farm enterprises. However, private farmers receive the same depressed product prices as do the farm enterprises, and their opportunities for investment are similarly constrained by low profitability and inability to borrow at commercial interest rates.

The opportunity for producers to sell their products at world trading prices (adjusted for quality and transport costs) is a key to agricultural recovery in Russia. There is fundamental disagreement, however, on how prices should be raised, whether through programs of direct government price support, or improvements in the functioning and competitiveness of agricultural markets. Until the reasons for depressed producer prices are better understood, interventions designed to increase prices are likely to fail or be very costly. For example, if depressed prices are due in part to monopoly in marketing and processing, then processors rather than producers would capture most of the payments under a program of price support, and there would be little public benefit to offset the substantial costs. At present, transport costs, local trade restrictions, and non-competitive behavior in processing are thought to contribute to depressed producer prices, but the relative importance of each and the geographical incidence is poorly understood.

Along with low prices, poorly developed financial services constrain agricultural recovery. Farm managers and private farmers reported that they were unable to finance working capital and investments at interest rates they felt they could afford. Although the commercial borrowing rate (at approximately 200% annually) was negative in real terms, managers felt that they would be unable to repay loans at that rate of interest. Most private farmers (nearly 70%) in the 1994 survey had access to some borrowing at interest rates below 30% annually. Managers did not report high levels of debt in 1994, but nonetheless reported that unavailability of affordable credit and repayment of existing debt constrained their operations. Virtually all debt is short-term, and must be repaid out of current earnings, or refinanced at uncertain rates.

At the end of 1994, most agricultural debt was either written off or refinanced as long-term debt at negative real rates, which is equivalent to a substantial write-off. Repeated write-offs undermine the establishment of sound banking practices in rural areas. Moreover, rural banking will be unattractive to the financial sector as long as there are few depositors with savings and many uncreditworthy borrowers. Recovery of agricultural earnings and deposits will thus be a first step toward improved financial services for the sector. Without this step, affordable credit will of necessity be only in the form of subsidized and directed credit, which is very often allocated through questionable procedures, and subsequently written off.

Rural social services are deteriorating for those who have remained in collectives, and for those who have left. Farm managers are cutting back on expenditures for social services and employee benefits, and employees report a decline in services and benefits. Despite the requirements of the relevant laws, there has been relatively little transfer of social assets to local governments, because most are reported to be unprepared to accept the financial and administrative responsibilities. Farm employees do not indicate that continued access to services and benefits is high on their list of reasons for remaining within the enterprises, perhaps because the level of benefits is low and declining. Attention to rural public services, including health, education, and infrastructure for utilities, water supply, transportation, and communication is needed. Provision of rural services should be largely self-financing, through taxes on rural residents, but tax proceeds will be inadequate as long as agricultural earnings are depressed. Improved agricultural earnings will thus create opportunities to improve rural social services, and, conversely, improved delivery of services will be unlikely if agriculture continues to decline.

* * *

The current farm structure should be recognized as transitional. Some of the large share-holding farms may survive as viable units, and others are likely to undergo further reorganization.

Some private farmers are likely to fail, as happens throughout the world, only to be replaced by new entrants to farming. Russian policy makers should accept the advisability of allowing different forms of farm organization to evolve in agriculture. The choice among different forms should be free and voluntary, and the producers should be guided in their decisions by market forces. Instead of raising barriers to withdrawal of land and assets in an attempt to avert by administrative means fragmentation of existing large-scale farm enterprises, the Russian land code should provide for orderly withdrawal, with due advance notification to the enterprise, and negotiation on the specific piece of land to be withdrawn. For example, shareholders could be given a specified period to file notice of intent to withdraw after harvest, and those intending to withdraw during a given year could negotiate with those remaining to identify mutually acceptable parcels.

Reorganization of farms must be accompanied by adjustments in the service sector, including provision of inputs, processing, and marketing. It is not enough to privatize monopolistic state-owned service firms. Competition must be enhanced among providers of services to agriculture, so that producers will no longer be linked to a single regional organization and will be able to choose freely among alternative suppliers, marketers, and processors. Primary producers can compete with foreign imports only if the domestic marketing and processing industry is competitive.

The findings of the present study suggest four major areas for further research, where information for sound decision making is lacking. First, a major study should be undertaken to measure the extent to which producer incentives are depressed, and to diagnose the relative importance of causative factors. Without a clearer understanding of the causes of depressed prices and the regional dispersion of producer prices, remedial measures are not likely to be effective. Second, the performance of agro-processing and farm-service firms recently privatized as whole units through closed share distribution to employees should be evaluated with regard to current and future competitiveness (price and quality of output;

distribution of earnings between wages and investment; processing margins and storage costs; opportunities for attracting foreign direct investment). The evaluation should lead to recommendations to improve competitiveness by reducing margins, if these are found to be high, and thus improve producer prices and earnings. Third, an empirical study of the impact of any proposed government program of price support on producer prices, farm incomes, and marketing margins should be undertaken, and program costs should be compared with the benefits. The results of such study should be publicly debated prior to adoption of any program of price support. Lastly, international evidence on farm size and its relation to efficiency should be assembled and analyzed in order to provide a foundation for an informed debate about the development of alternative forms of farm organization in Russia.

1. Russian Agriculture: 1992-1994[1]

Changes in land tenure and in the organization and status of the traditional large-scale farms are visible components of the agricultural reforms that began in Russia at the end of 1991, following the dissolution of the Soviet Union. Reform in the agricultural sector also encompasses changes in the trade regime, in producer incentives, and in farm finances, all of which have significant impacts on the overall performance of agriculture. The various elements of agricultural reform are surveyed in this chapter in order to clarify the sectoral context in which the present study was undertaken.

Recent Changes in Land Tenure and Farm Organization

During the three years from 1992 through 1994, Russia embarked upon a large scale transfer of ownership of agricultural land from the state to the enterprises that work the land. A lesser, but still substantial amount of land was transferred to individual private ownership. Table 1.1 shows changes in land holding by type of user. In 1994, state agricultural enterprises held less than 18% of agricultural land, down from close to 60% prior to 1991. Agricultural enterprises not in the state sector held 70% of agricultural land, up from 40% prior to 1991. Individuals, including private farmers and holders of household plots, held 12% of agricultural land, up from less than 2% before 1991.

Land holding is not synonymous with ownership, since some individual landholders or non-state agricultural enterprises do not yet own their land. The data in Table 1.1, however, accurately reflect the primary development in land reform during the period 1992-1994; i.e., the expansion in the share of land held and managed by agricultural enterprises of various types outside the state sector.

Table 1.1. Land Holding by Type of User in Russia: 1991-1995 (% of agricultural land)

Sector and Enterprise Type	Jan. 1991	Jan. 1994	Jan. 1995
State sector	58.2	17.6	16.5
Collective/cooperative sector	40.0	70.5	71.1
Incl. shareholding enterprises	0.3	52.5	54.2
Private sector	1.8	11.9	12.5
Private farms	0.0	5.0	5.3
Associations of private farms	0.0	2.2	2.4
Household plots	1.4	2.8	2.9
Other	0.4	1.9	1.9
Total agricultural land, mill. ha	**213.0**	**210.1**	

Table 1.2. Share of Land and Production by Farm Category in 1994 (% total)

	Enterprises	Private Farms	Household Plots
Agricultural land	**88.1**	**5.0**	**2.8**
Value of output	**60.0**	**2.0**	**38.0**
Grain production	94.2	5.1	0.7
Sunflower	88.2	10.2	1.6
Sugarbeets	95.8	3.5	0.7
Potatoes	11.0	0.9	88.1
Meat	56.0	0.1	43.0
Milk	60.0	0.1	39.0
Eggs	71.0	0.1	28.0

Several indicators of the relative size of the farm enterprise sector, private farms, and the household sector are shown in Table 1.2. The household sector continues to account for a high proportion of gross agricultural product, while the contribution of independent private farms to output is still very low (and even less than their share of land holdings). The enterprise sector traditionally

---

[1] The sources of data for tables and figures are listed at the end of the chapter.

dominates the production of grain and technical crops, while the household plots are the major producer of potatoes and vegetables. Private farmers also appear to concentrate on grain, sunflower, and sugarbeets as their main cash crops, with much less emphasis on potatoes. Livestock products are produced in roughly equal proportions by enterprises and households, with very little production by private farmers.

Almost all state and collective farms had re-registered by January 1994, in compliance with the new laws and decrees (Table 1.3). Most of the agricultural producer enterprises in 1994 were shareholding farms of the closed or limited liability variety or collective and state farms that decided to retain their former status. The land and assets of these enterprises are now in most cases owned by the enterprises, and the enterprises in turn are owned by shareholders, who are employees or former employees (pensioners) entitled to participate in the distribution of land and asset shares by the former entity. The shareholding enterprises are thus collectives in a truer sense than were the collectives of the pre-reform period, which in practice differed little from state farms.

Table 1.3. Agricultural Enterprises of Different Organizational Forms (in thousands)

	Jan. 1993	Jan. 1994
Re-registered farms	**19.7**	**24.3**
Percent of total	**77%**	**95%**
Retained former status during re-registration	7.0	8.4
Closed shareholding firms, limited liability partnerships	8.6	11.5
Open shareholding firms	0.3	0.3
Agricultural producers' cooperatives	1.7	1.9
Associations of private farmers	0.7	0.9
Registered private farmers	182.8	270.0
Private farms created through enterprise reorganization	43.6	81.6

The survey results reported later in this study show in detail the ownership of assets and economic behavior in a sample of agricultural enterprises and private farmers. In general the

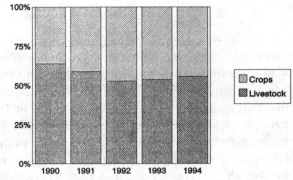

Fig. 1.1. Changes in Product Mix in Russia, 1990-1994

Based on gross agricultural product in current prices.

shareholding enterprises of various types resemble each other in internal structure. In size and economic behavior they have much in common with the state and collective farms that were their immediate predecessors. Some internal changes have taken place; in particular the household plots have expanded (doubling their share of agricultural land between 1990 and 1993; see Table 1.1), and the product and input mix in the enterprise sector has changed somewhat in response to new relative prices and financial constraints (Fig. 1.1).

The closed shareholding farm is the preferred organizational form among the enterprises that re-registered (see Tables 1.1 and 1.3). It is closed in the sense that only employees and pensioners can own shares, which are not tradable outside the farm. There are several types of closed shareholding farms in accordance with the Russian Civil Code. A *joint stock company* is comprised usually of most or all members and employees of the former collective or state farm. The joint stock company must be registered with federal financial authorities and must issue stock. A *limited liability partnership* is formed by contribution of members' shares to the charter capital of the enterprise. Members formally have voting rights on routine managerial decisions, unlike shareholders in a joint stock company, where voting in general is limited to choice of management and major decisions. In practice, many limited liability partnerships and joint stock companies are of similar size and internal organization, and are functionally indistinguishable. Liability of members in both types of organizations does not exceed the value of the individual's share capital. Relatively few agricultural *producers' cooperatives* have been formed (1900 nationwide in 1994), in part because legal issues are unclear pending passage of a law on cooperatives, and in part because many enterprises in which members prefer cooperative production have remained collective farms. In *associations of private farmers*, the individual members should be registered private farmers who have formed an association in order to perform tasks jointly. In practice, associations exist in which members are not individually registered private farmers, and in which production is managed collectively. In other associations, production is largely private, and activities of the association include shared access to nondivisible infrastructure or joint purchasing and marketing.

The creation of the new enterprise sector in Russia has been a result of the design of the program of land reform and farm restructuring. The enterprises at present own land and assets because the shareholding farm is the vehicle through which property rights are passed to the individuals who invested labor in agriculture over the decades of Soviet rule. In some cases the enterprises have not yet implemented procedures for assigning property rights to individuals, and the rights remain in joint ownership. In other cases rights have been assigned to individuals, and the individuals have reassigned rights on a temporary or contractual basis to the larger enterprises with which they have been historically associated. In some cases, the original enterprise has reorganized into a number of smaller units through regrouping of members' shares. In general land and asset rights have stayed with the enterprises because procedures for further allocation have not yet been implemented on a large scale. In addition, collectives have been allowed to remain as units even in cases in which they are not financially viable because bankruptcy procedures have not been well defined and enforced.

Property rights temporarily vested in enterprises between 1992 and 1994 have thus tended to stay there. Where the enterprise is still in the process of reorganization, or has not yet begun to reorganize, the enterprise has a temporary custodial property right. Individual shareholders have the right to withdraw real property during the reorganization. Where the enterprise has completed formal reorganization, however, individuals in most cases do not have a free right to withdraw property.

Land held by enterprises is most often registered as jointly owned property, and under the Civil Code disposition of private property jointly owned by several owners requires permission of all owners. Any enterprise can elect to undergo a full reorganization, at which time shares can be passed again to owners for their disposition, either by exit or reinvestment. The law at present, however, attaches an unconditional right to exit with land only during the process of reorganization. The legal requirement established at the beginning of the reforms in December 1991 that all collective and state farms vote on reorganization and re-register has been fulfilled formally, but has brought little actual change in the size and organizational structure of enterprises.

Sectoral Performance During the Period 1991-1994

The initial phase of land reform and creation of the new enterprise sector has taken place during a period of absolute and relative decline in agriculture. Gross agricultural output measured in constant prices fell 24% between 1990 and 1994 (Table 1.4). Agriculture's share of GDP fell from around 15% in 1990 to 6% in 1994.

Table 1.4. Share of Agriculture in GDP and Index of Gross Agricultural Output in Russia: 1990-1994

	Share of agriculture in GDP, %	*Gross agricultural output*		
		Total	*Livestock*	*Crops*
1990	15.3	100.0	100.0	100.0
1991	11.9	95.5	92.7	100.5
1992	8.6	86.5	81.7	95.1
1993	8.4	82.7	77.2	92.4
1994	6.3	75.3	71.0	83.2

Reasons for the decline include loss of protected markets, disruption of normal trading relations, declining domestic demand due to declining consumer incomes, reduction of traditional subsidies, and deterioration in sectoral terms of trade. The rise of the service sector in Russia has also contributed to the declining share of the traditional productive sectors.

Both the crop and livestock sectors have declined, as shown in Table 1.4. The initial shock to profitability was felt most in the livestock sector, as the cost of feed increased and consumers cut back on purchases of meat. Farm enterprises responded to the decline in profitability of meat production by reducing animal numbers, and their herd reduction was not compensated by the increase in livestock numbers in the household sector (Table 1.5). The decline in the aggregate number of cows was less than that for cattle in general (Fig. 1.2), reflecting increased production of milk for own consumption in the household sector, and the attractiveness of dairying as a source of regular cash income in both enterprise and household sectors. The proportion of cows in the private sector increased, although the share of private farms in dairying is still very small.

The decline in agriculture has been a common feature of transitional economies throughout Central and Eastern Europe and the former Soviet Union (Table 1.6). All the countries have been affected in varying degrees by the changes in the economic and sectoral environment. In addition, some countries have suffered from natural disasters and civil unrest. Although Russia's agricultural decline has been less severe than in some countries, it continues in 1995, while in a number of Central and Eastern European countries agricultural production appears to have bottomed out in 1993 and certain relative gains were registered in 1994 and 1995.

Profitability and Incentives

The decline in production in Russia has been in part a response to falling profitability of the sector. Although the decline in profitability is acutely felt and widely noted, it is poorly documented. The old accounting procedures do not reflect the impact of inflation on cost of inputs and

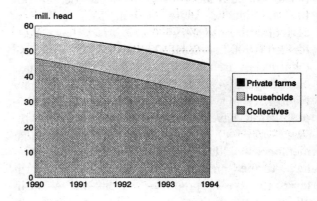

Fig. 1.2a. Livestock in Russia: Cattle

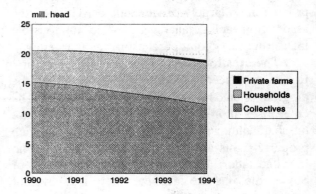

Fig. 1.2b. Livestock in Russia: Cows

the inflation adjusted value of depreciation. Reported profitability may thus be positive and even substantial when the farms have difficulty meeting current wage and tax obligations and are unable to finance purchase of inputs for the future production year.

Although actual data on sectoral profitability are at present incomplete, available data on producer incentives suggest that profitability is likely to be low due to depressed producer prices. The erosion of farm profitability is often attributed in the Russian press and analytical literature to a violation of price parity, or an opening of the price scissors. The concept of parity or the price scissors refers to change in an index of agricultural product prices relative to input prices or industrial prices more generally. Index numbers of prices for farm inputs and outputs are shown in Table 1.7, and they confirm that domestic intersectoral terms of trade moved against primary agriculture between 1991 and 1994. Thus, while the prices of all industrial inputs and services for agriculture increased by a factor of nearly 1400 between 1990 and 1994, aggregate crop prices increased by a factor of 550 and prices of livestock products only by a factor of 330.

The concept of price parity was used in the past in market economies as an analytical tool to measure changes in relative prices. As developed market economies became increasingly dynamic and open to trade, price parity ceased to be a useful normative measure, since relative prices in dynamic open economies change rapidly in response to changes in technology, trading opportunities, and consumer demand. Moreover, when relative prices are distorted in the base year, as was the case in Russia in 1990, prior to reforms, price parity calculations perpetuate the initial distortion.

Table 1.5. Livestock Numbers and Sectoral Structure of the Herd in Russia (million head and percent, end of year data)

	1990	1991	1992	1993	1994
Cattle, mill. head	**57.1**	**54.7**	**52.2**	**48.9**	**44.9**
Enterprises	47.2	43.9	40.2	36.3	31.9
Households+Farmers	9.9	10.8	12.0	12.6	13.0
Cows, mill. head	**20.6**	**20.6**	**20.2**	**19.8**	**19.0**
Enterprises	15.3	14.8	13.7	12.8	11.6
Households+Farmers	5.3	5.8	6.5	7.0	7.4
	1990	1991	1992	1993	1994
Cattle, %	**100**	**100**	**100**	**100**	**100**
Enterprises	83	80	77	74	71
Households	17	20	22	25	27
Farmers	--	0	1	1	2
Cows, %	**100**	**100**	**100**	**100**	**100**
Enterprises	74	72	68	65	61
Households	26	28	32	34	37
Farmers	--	0	0	1	2

Table 1.6. Index of Gross Agricultural Output in Economies in Transition (1990 = 100)

	1991	1992	1993	1994		1991	1992	1993	1994
Former Soviet Republics					*Baltic Countries*				
Azerbaidjan	100	75	64	55	Estonia	96	78	72	65
Armenia	100	87	108	111	Latvia	96	84	70	53
Belarus	95	86	90	77	Lithuania	96	73	67	82
Georgia	66	55	35	31					
Kazakhstan	90	91	86	72	*Central and Eastern Europe*				
Kyrgyzstan	90	86	77	65	Albania	79	93	106	115
Moldova	90	76	81	58	Bulgaria	100	88	72	75
Russia	95	86	83	75	Czech Republic	91	80	79	81
Tadjikistan	96	70	67	50	Slovakia	96	69	72	75
Turkmenistan	96	87	101	103	Hungary	94	75	68	69
Uzbekistan	99	93	94	93	Poland	98	88	89	83
Ukraine	87	80	82	68	Romania	101	87	99	104

Table 1.7. Index Numbers of Prices for Agricultural Outputs and Inputs in Russia (average for year, ratio of the prior year)

	1991	*1992*	*1993*	*1994*	*1994 to 1990*
Outputs:					
Crop products	**1.9**	**17.6**	**6.1**	**2.7**	**551**
Grains	1.5	21.8	5.3	2.2	381
Oil seeds	1.8	21.0	4.3	3.3	536
Potatoes	3.4	9.0	6.9	4.2	887
Livestock products	**1.6**	**6.2**	**10.4**	**3.2**	**330**
Beef	1.5	4.8	11.7	2.6	219
Pork	1.5	7.2	13.5	3.0	437
Milk	1.4	6.9	8.6	3.3	274
Farm Inputs:					
All industrial inputs and services	**1.9**	**16.2**	**10.7**	**4.2**	**1383**
Tractors	2.3	21.9	11.0	4.0	2216
Fertilizer	1.7	12.8	10.7	6.5	1513
Fuel	1.3	34.6	11.3	3.4	1728
Mixed feed	2.1	17.9	8.6	3.7	1196

Table 1.8. Domestic and Border Prices in Russia: 1993-1994 (US$ per ton, at market exchange rate)*

	1993			*1994*		
	Border	*Domestic*	*Ratio#*	*Border*	*Domestic*	*Ratio#*
Food Commodities						
Wheat (Import)	147-165	64 [a]	0.44-0.39	154	66 [a]	0.43
Corn (Import)	142			159		
Sugar (Import)	397	305	0.77	360	268	0.74
Beef (Import)	1365	586[b]	0.42	1260	666[b]	0.52
Pork (Import)	1365	918[b]	0.68	1260	1200[b]	0.95
Farm Inputs						
Anhydrous anmonia (Export)	81	19	0.23	108	55	0.51
Nitrogen fertilizer (Export)	69	17	0.25	80	49	0.61
Potassium fertilizer (Export)	65	11	0.17	74	46	0.62
Phosphatic fertilizer (Export)	121	29	0.24	158	94	0.59
Tractors (Export) (piece)	3689	2692	0.73	2708	4923	1.83
Diesel fuel	153	73	0.48	123	124	1.01

*   Average 1993 domestic prices converted at 1000 rubles/US$, average 1994 domestic prices converted at 2205 rubles/US$.
\#   Ratio of domestic to border prices.
[a]   Domestic prices paid by procurement organization for general grain, which consists largely of wheat.
[b]   Prices converted to slaughter weight with conversion factor approximately 2 relative to live weight price.

Price parity has been replaced in developed market economies by several analytical tools that measure domestic price distortions relative to prices on world markets, rather than relative to domestic prices at a point in the past. These concepts include nominal protection (the value of production in domestic prices relative to the value in world prices), effective protection (value added in domestic prices relative to value added in world trading prices), and producer subsidy equivalents (value of production at world trading prices plus all direct and indirect subsidies relative to value of production at domestic prices). These indicators provide a progressively more comprehensive view of the degree of sectoral subsidy or taxation relative to world trading prices.

The internationally accepted indicators have not yet been calculated for Russia, but some data relevant to the calculations are shown in Table 1.8. These data indicate that although domestic prices of agricultural products and inputs moved closer to world levels in 1994, they still remained much lower in most cases, particularly for grains.

From the data in Table 1.8 it appears that earnings of Russian producers would improve if input and output prices moved to world levels. In other words, the current price regime constitutes indirect net taxation of the sector relative to world trading prices. While transfers through the budget and banking system are still substantial and debt writeoffs continue to be practiced, producer subsidy equivalents are likely to be negative when domestic prices for important products are as low as 50% of border prices (see Table 1.8).

Low producer prices may derive from regulatory barriers to trade, imperfections in product markets, high transaction costs, or a combination of all of these. Factors depressing product prices at the national level, such as administrative pricing, state orders, and barriers to export, have been removed. The effort to understand determinants of producer prices must therefore focus on the sub-national level

The pattern of purchase prices over time and the reported geographic dispersion of producer prices suggest that the liberalization of producer prices has not been effective or complete. For example, in 1993 milk producers were paid on average 9200 rubles per ton ($9.20) in Ul'yanovsk Province on the middle Volga, and 19,100 rubles per ton ($19.1) in the neighboring Tatarstan. These prices compared to 35,000-50,000 rubles ($35-$50) per ton of milk in other provinces of the mid-Volga region. Both Ul'yanovsk and Tatarstan have well publicized local policies to maintain low consumer prices for food, and these policies appear to be funded in large part by implicit taxes on local producers. Local policies and local barriers to trade are probably among the chief constraints depressing producer prices.

Some analysts within Russia have argued that the solution to severely depressed producer prices lies in a federal program of price support, according to which the federal government would be a buyer of last resort at the border price. The proposal would be difficult to implement because the federal government at present lacks budgetary funds for agricultural price support. Aside from the fiscal constraints, however, the proposal has a more fundamental flaw. Measures to remove distortions in producer prices should be based on an understanding of what is causing the distortions. If producer prices are low due to market imperfections and/or local regulations, it is unlikely that a federal program of price support would improve prices at the farm gate. Instead the large sums spent through the program would be diverted to those currently benefiting from the price distortions, and producers would see little change. A careful study quantifying the factors that contribute to the gap between domestic and border prices in major producing regions of Russia should be undertaken for grains, oilseeds, meat, and milk. The objective of such a study should be to identify measures that can improve producer incentives by improving the functioning of markets.

Farm Finances, Debt, and Investment

The deteriorating terms of trade in agriculture and the steep decline in production have apparently had a severe effect on farm profits and on the availability of resources for investment and growth. Investment in productive assets in agriculture virtually ceased in 1994. Total reported agricultural investment in 1994 was around 8% of its 1990 level (Table 1.9). The decline of 92% in agricultural investment between 1990 and 1994 was much greater than the decline for the economy as a whole, where total investment in productive assets in 1994 had dropped to 26% of the 1990 level. Agriculture's share of total productive investment fell from its traditional high of 20%-25% in 1990 and 1991 to less than 10% in 1994.

The sectoral contraction evident from the dramatic decline in production and investment has apparently reduced the financing needs of Russian agriculture and enabled it to avoid the crushing buildup of debt that typically accompanies declining profits. The net indebtedness of agriculture in December 1994 was around 15% of total agricultural product (Table 1.10), practically equal to the debt ratio of industry (13%). The use of short-term non-bank credit in agriculture (suppliers' credit and other current obligations and arrears) did not increase significantly during 1994: the average payment period of accounts payable (including obligations to suppliers, the government, and the payroll) remained at a level of about 65 days, as shown in Fig. 1.3.

Table 1.9. Index of Investment in Russia: 1990-1994 (1990=100)

	1990	1991	1992	1993	1994
Total investment	100	84	51	75	33
Total investment in productive assets	100	82	47	41	26
Investment in agricultural productive assets	100	95	33	21	8
Share of agricultural investment in total productive investment	22%	26%	16%	12%	9%

Table 1.10. Financial Position of Russian Agriculture (billion rubles)

	Agriculture		Industry	
	1 Dec 1994	1 Mar 1995	1 Dec 1994	1 Mar 1995
1 Outstanding bank debt and loans	9078	10537	29364	37042
2 Accounts payable*	7469	9874	117050	151223
3 Accounts receivable**	4113	4372	102933	126379
4 Net indebtedness 1+2-3	12434	16039	43481	61886
5 Total product (current prices)	81601	NA	344430	NA
6 Net indebtedness over total product 4/5	15%	NA	13%	NA

* Includes suppliers, the government, workers' payroll, and others.
** Includes customers and other receivables.

Table 1.11. Working Capital Position of Russian Agriculture (billion rubles)

	Agriculture			Industry		
	1 Jan 94	1 Dec 94	1 Mar 95	1 Jan 94	1 Dec 94	1 Mar 95
1 Payable to suppliers	1583	4808	5594	22615	71337	84271
2 Receivable from customers	1497	3253	3393	27349	83451	102282
3 Working capital ratio 2/1	0.95	0.68	0.61	1.21	1.17	1.21
% overdue payables	34%	52%	56%	41%	57%	51%
% overdue receivables	41%	50%	46%	45%	58%	55%

In addition to unfavorable terms of trade between the prices of inputs and the prices of products, agriculture also faces, like the rest of the economy, an unfavorable disparity between payment obligations to suppliers and collections from customers. Compared to 65 days of credit from suppliers, farms grant around 75 days of credit to the customers (up from 70 days in the first quarter of 1994; see Fig. 1.3). This finding is consistent with the complaints voiced by Russian

Fig. 1.3. Average Payment and Collection Period
(Agriculture, Industry, Transport, and Construction)

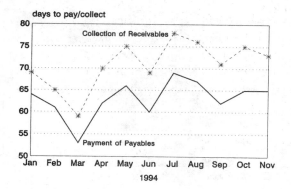

farmers and farm managers that they are squeezed from both ends by monopolistic suppliers demanding quick payment if not prepayment for inputs, and monopolistic processors unreasonably stretching the payment for products delivered. Overall, however, this mismatch in payment terms does not appear to be a direct source of difficulties for the sector, as there is no evidence of rapid buildup of receivables that need to be financed.

On the contrary, the level of receivables from customers for farm products is declining relative to the level of supplier credit (Table 1.11). The ratio of customer receivables to supplier credit dropped from nearly 1 at the end of 1993 to 0.6 in the first quarter of 1995 (while the corresponding ratio for industry remained at a level of 1.2). Contraction of activities normally produces roughly the same decrease in both accounts receivable and accounts payable, and the relative increase of accounts payable in Russian agriculture suggests that farms increasingly rely on supplier credit and other arrears as a general source of financing.

The fact that accounts receivable are less than accounts payable points to a negative working capital position in Russian agriculture and casts doubts on agriculture's ability to repay its current debt, which is typically covered by collections from customers. The increase in the proportion of overdue payables from 34% of all payables to suppliers in January 1994 to over 50% in the first quarter of 1995 also suggests evidence of impending repayment difficulties (although this

level of overdue accounts is not much different from that in industry; Table 1.11). Recognizing the liquidity squeeze of agriculture, the Russian government in December 1994 yielded to pressure from the farming lobby and forgave half the accrued interest obligations (6 trillion rubles), while rescheduling the repayment of the principal (another 6 trillion) from short-term to 10 years. The forgiven amount was roughly equal to one third of debt outstanding as of Dec. 1, 1994, or half the net indebtedness of the sector (Table 1.10). After the writeoff, agriculture's net indebtedness dropped from 15% of gross product to less than 8% (compared to 13% for industry).

The incomplete data currently available on aggregate farm finances leave many questions open. According to anecdotal reports, finances at the farm level deteriorated in 1994, and many farms were unable to pay wages, social security, and taxes. More detailed work on farm finance at the aggregate and at the farm level will be needed. Farm finance is an issue integrally linked to farm restructuring because farm debt must be allocated along with assets during restructuring. Moreover, farms with negative net worth may require special procedures for reorganization, and these procedures are not yet developed.

Marketing of Output

The traditional structure of agricultural marketing, with its reliance on state procurement organs, is undergoing a major change. In 1994, producers shifted away from the formerly state-owned procurement firms, which have a very poor record of timely payment, and sought alternative marketing channels, as shown in Table 1.12.

The other channels reported in Table 1.12 include local cash markets, barter deals, and distributions in kind in lieu of cash wages. Prices for grain on local markets or in barter deals in 1994 were lower than the prices paid by large procurement firms (Table 1.13). Yet producers in 1994 were willing to accept lower prices for grain to reduce the risk of contractual noncompliance and shorten the time between delivery and receipt of payment. In contrast to grain, prices for livestock products were reported to be higher in direct marketing channels in 1994 than in procurement contracts.

The shift in marketing behavior in 1994 has resulted in increased activity on local markets, and an increased volume of transactions in kind, such as wage payments in kind to agricultural workers. Although agricultural wages are poorly measured under current conditions, there is little doubt that real wages are falling absolutely and relative to wages in other sectors. In February 1995 agricultural workers were the lowest paid of all sectors, and earned just 33% of average wage in industry and one quarter of that in food processing industry (Fig. 1.4). The methodology for calculation of reported wages includes estimates of earnings in kind, but does not include nonpayment due to arrears. In 1990 agricultural wages in the RSFSR calculated on the same basis were approximately equal to average industrial wages.

Agricultural Trade

The decline in sectoral production and earnings has led to increased pressure for protection against imports. Agricultural wages have fallen, production has declined, and farm finances deteriorated at the same time that food imports of some highly visible commodities, such as meat, have increased. Russian imports of meat and poultry from outside the former Soviet Union in 1994 were just under 800,000 tons, almost at the level of meat imports for the entire Soviet Union

Fig. 1.4. Wages by Economic Sector in Russia

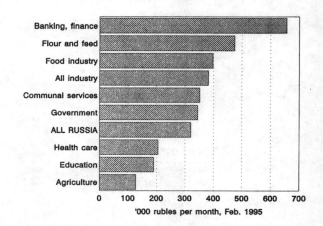

'000 rubles per month, Feb. 1995

prior to the reform, when meat consumption was still subsidized.

Imports are highly concentrated in Moscow, where they comprise a high proportion of food marketed. Moscow is atypical of the entire country, however, and imports in general constitute a modest share of domestic consumption of most products. Increased agricultural protection was nonetheless prominent in the policy debate throughout 1994. Tariffs were increased on average by 2% effective July 1, 1995, and a special increase of 10% in the value added tax on imported food was also introduced. The political climate has been supportive of increased protection for food, although the trade data show that food imports are lower than they were in the pre-reform period.

Table 1.12. Change in Marketing Channels in Russia: 1991-1994 (% of all marketed output)

	1991		*1993*		*1994*	
	Procurement organs	*Other channels*	*Procurement orgrans*	*Other channels*	*Procurement organs*	*Other channels*
Grains	64	36	63	37	34	66
Oilseeds	89	11	48	52	12	88
Sugarbeets	100	0	98	2	67	33
Potatoes	69	31	52	48	37	67
Vegetables	84	16	71	29	59	41
Meat	84	16	79	21	70	30
Milk	98	2	97	3	93	7

Table 1.13. Prices in Various Marketing Channels in Russia: Third Quarter 1994 ('000 ruble/ton)

	Weighted average	Procurement organs	Direct marketing	Internal distribution	Barter
Grain	106.0	140.9	85.8	53.3	89.3
Potatoes	289.4	334.4	286.9	198.5	288.1
Vegetables	570.8	557.3	617.3	484.9	499.0
Beef, live weight	723.5	709.8	799.3	714.8	768.9
Pork, live weight	1320.4	1335.7	1402.1	1158.8	1104.2
Milk	142.9	137.6	252.2	199.9	194.3

Table 1.14. Russian Imports: 1990-1994 (billion US$)

	All Commodities			Food		
	Total	Former Soviet republics	Other	Total	Former Soviet republics	Other
1990	153.8	72.0	81.8	33.9	17.3	16.6
1991	149.1	104.6	44.5	34.5	22.1	12.4
1992	45.8	8.8	37.0	10.1	0.5	9.6
1993	35.8	9.0	26.8	6.9	1.1	5.9
1994	38.6	10.3	28.3	8.9	1.4	7.5

Agricultural imports in aggregate are reported to have declined by more then two-thirds throughout the reform period (Table 1.14). Food imports from non-FSU partners increased by 27% in 1994 relative to 1993, and comprised $7.5 billion, but were still less than half the recorded Russian imports from non-FSU partners in 1990. The volume and value of food imports from FSU partners has fallen very substantially, from over $17 billion in 1990 (roughly equal to imports from non-FSU partners) to less than $2 billion in 1993 and 1994. Table 1.15 shows imports from outside the former Soviet Union in physical units. The decline in grain and sugar imports explains much of the fall in the value of imports, despite significant growth in imports of livestock products.

The relatively small volume of agricultural imports and the large gap between domestic and border prices (see Table 1.8) suggest that increased agricultural protection is not likely to raise earnings of Russian primary producers. When the gap between domestic and border prices is as high as that displayed in Table 1.8, additional protection at the border will have little if any impact on producer prices. Imported foodstuffs are processed or semi-processed. To the extent that higher protection raises consumer prices, it is likely to increase the margins between farm-gate and retail prices, rather than increase farm-gate prices. If the food processing industry is monopolistic, increased protection will strengthen the monopolies.

Table 1.15. Food Imports to Russia from Non-FSU Countries (thousand tons)

	1992	1993	1994
Meat	288	85	387
Poultry	46	74	411
Butter	25	70	171
Citrus	42	172	869
Tea	47	55	98
Sugar, unrefined	2137	1667	1203
Sugar, refined	1554	1442	1083
Grains	30386	11450	2096

Monopoly is not the only structural issue of importance to the performance of the food processing industry. Many of the processing plants were privatized in closed distributions to employees, and they have become essentially worker-managed firms. Closed worker-managed firms have problems familiar from the theoretical literature and from past experience in the former Yugoslavia. In worker-managed firms employees have incentives to distribute profits as wages, rather than reinvest in the firm, and the firms are forced to rely on relatively high levels of debt for financing.

Reported wages in the food industry, as shown in Fig. 1.4, are quite high. Agricultural producers have frequently pointed to the disparity in earnings between agricultural workers and food industry workers, and presented the gap as evidence of monopsony power in the food industry. Unless labor can move freely between the two subsectors and the skill requirements of the two types of employment are the same, there is little reason to accept wage gaps as evidence of monopsony. If wages in food processing are elevated, however, relative to equilibrium levels in an integrated labor market, this may be due either to monopsony power or to asset stripping on the part of employees in labor managed firms. Both monopsony power and asset stripping or underinvestment in the food processing industry on the part of the new employee-owners will impede growth and competitiveness of primary production.

* * *

Russian land reform and farm restructuring through 1994 have resulted in stronger land tenure rights of the enterprise sector. Changes in the size, internal structure, and economic behavior of enterprises have been modest to date. The slow pace of change is due in part to deficiencies in the legal framework for reorganization and to delay in design of readily operational models of restructuring. In part the continued strength of the traditional enterprise sector derives from poor producer incentives and lack of development of product and input markets. Under prevailing prices, earnings outside the collectives are insufficient to attract financing for initial start-up capital and operating expenses. Although severe problems remain in supply of financial services to agriculture, even a well developed commercial financial sector would be reluctant to finance agricultural activities under the sectoral incentives prevailing in 1993 and 1994. Improved producer incentives resulting from more competitive and efficient marketing and processing, and better and cheaper access to national and international markets will be needed in order for viable commercial farms to emerge through continued progress in land reform and farm restructuring.

Russian land reform and farm restructuring made a promising start between 1992-1994, but much further change lies ahead if a competitive and efficient farm structure is to emerge. The changes accomplished so far have taken place in a sectoral economic environment that depressed farm earnings and asset values. The sectoral environment in the future will improve as farm product prices increase. Because a substantial improvement in sectoral incentives lies ahead, it is important that land and farm assets not be prematurely locked into the collective and corporate structure that emerged in 1992-1994. Continued positive evolution of farm structure in Russia will require that the government put emphasis on the following areas: (i) design of a workable mechanism for exit or separation from shareholding enterprises, so that land and assets are not locked in the units created in the first round of formal restructuring; and (ii) enhanced functioning of markets in the agricultural sector so that producer incentives improve to reflect undistorted market opportunities.

List of Data Sources in Chapter 1

Fig. 1.1: *Statisticheskii byulleten' No. 1(APK)*, Goskomstat RF, Moscow, 1995.

Fig. 1.2: *Rossiya 1994. Ekonomicheskaya kon'yunktura*, Tsentr Ekonomicheskoi Kon'yunktury, Moscow, December 1994.

Fig. 1.3: *Sotsial'no-ekonomisheskoe polozhenie Rossii 1994*, Goskomstat RF, Moscow, p. 104.

Fig. 1.4: *Sotsial'no-ekonomicheskoe polozhenie Rossii, Yanvar'-Mart 1995*, Groskomstat RF, Moscow, 1995.

Table 1.1: *Narodnoe khozyaistvo Rossiiskoi Federatsii 1992*, Goskomstat RF, Moscow, 1993; *Rossiiskii statisticheskii ezhegodnik 1994*, Goskomstat RF, Moscow, 1995.

Table 1.2: *Rossiiskii statisticheskii ezhegodnik 1994*, Goskomstat RF, Moscow, 1995, p. 346.

Table 1.3: *Statisticheskii byulleten' No. 1 (APK)*; *Osnovnye pokazateli funktsionirovaniia APK Rossiiskoi federatsii v 1994g.*, Moscow, 1995

Table 1.4: *Rossiya 1994. Ekonomicheskaya kon'yunktura*, Tsentr Ekonomicheskoi Kon'yunktury, Moscow, December 1994.

Table 1.5: *Rossiya 1994. Ekonomicheskaya kon'yunktura*, Tsentr Ekonomicheskoi Kon'yunktury, Moscow, December 1994.

Table 1.6: *Strany-chleny SNG v 1993 g.*, Moscow, 1994; *Strany-chleny SNG v 1993 g. (Kratkii spravochnik)*, Moscow, 1994; *Strany-chleny SNG v 1994 g. (Kratkii spravochnik predvaritel'nykh statisticheskikh itogov)*, Moscow, 1994; *Narodnoe khoziaistvo SSSR 1990*, Goskomstat, Moscow, 1991; *Statisticheskii byulleten' No. 5 (93)*, Moscow, February 1995; *Agricultural Policies, Markets and Trade in the Central and Eastern European countries, Selected New Independent States, Mongolia and China: Monitoring and Outlook 1995*, OECD, Paris, 1995.

Table 1.7: *Tseny v Rossiiskoi Federatsii*, Goskomstat RF, Moscow 1995.

Table 1.8: *Tseny v Rossiskoi Federatsii*, Goskomstat RF, Moscow, 1994 and 1995; *Rossiya 1994. Ekonomicheskaya kon'yunktura*, Tsentr Ekonomicheskoi Kon'yunktury, Moscow, December 1994; *Statisticheskii byulleten' SNG No. 5*, 1995.

Table 1.9: *Rossiiskii statisticheskii ezhegodnik 1994*; *Sotsial'no-ekonomicheskoe polozhenie Rossii 1994*; *Statisticheskii byulleten' No.1 (APK)*, Goskomstat RF, Moscow, 1995.

Table 1.10: *Sotsial'no-ekonomishesskoe polozhenie Rossii 1994*; *Sotsial'no-ekonomicheskoe polozhenie Rossii Yanvar'-Mart 1995*; *Statisticheskii byulleten' No. 1 (APK)*, Goskomstat RF, Moscow, 1995.

Table 1.11: *Rossiiskii statisticheskii ezhegodnik 1994*; *Sotsial'no-ekonomisheskoe polozhenie Rossii 1994*; *Sotsial'no-ekonomicheskoe polozhenie Rossii Yanvar'-Mart 1995*, Goskomstat RF, Moscow, 1995.

Table 1.12: *Statisticheskii byulleten' No. 1 (APK)*, *Osnovnye pokazateli funktsionirovaniya agro-promyshlennogo kompleksa Rossiiskoi Federatsii v 1994 godu*, Goskomstat RF, Moscow, 1995.

Table 1.13: *Rossiya 1994. Ekonomicheskaya kon'yunktura*, Tsentr Ekonomicheskoi Kon'yunktury, Moscow, December 1994.

Table 1.14: *Rossiya 1994. Ekonomicheskaya kon'yunktura*, Tsentr Ekonomicheskoi Kon'yunktury, Moscow, December 1994; *Sotsial'no-ekonomicheskoe polozhenie Rossii 1994*, Goskomstat RF, Moscow, 1995.

Table 1.15: *Rossiiskii statisticheskii ezhegodnik 1994*, Goskomstat RF, Moscow, 1995; *Rossiiskaya Federatsiya v 1992 g.*, Goskomstat RF, Moscow, 1993; *Statisticheskii byulleten' No. 1 (APK)*, Goskomstat RF, Moscow, 1995.

2. The Legal Framework for Land Markets and Reorganization of Farms

Land law in a market economy defines and protects property rights in land, and creates legal conditions under which rights can be transferred through markets. During Russia's transitional period, the land law and laws governing farm reorganization are interrelated, since they pertain to two components of the reform process that are closely linked and interdependent. This section reviews the legal framework for both components as of 1995 and early 1996. For a discussion of previous phases, see Brooks and Lerman (1994).

Russian Land Law

The early stage of land reform and farm restructuring, prior to 1994, proceeded in the absence of constitutional guarantees for land owners, and was directed largely by presidential decrees. The new Russian Constitution effective since December 1993, and the Civil Code effective since January 1995, safeguard the right to private property and private land ownership and provide the legal basis for other legislative acts or decrees. Yet a number of old laws still remain on the books that are not consistent with the Constitution and the Civil Code, and the legal framework is under continuing revision and review.

Three aspects of land law; i.e., *ownership*, *transactions*, and *mortgage*, are critical if agriculture is to function efficiently in a market economy. In these three areas the Russian legal framework is at present based on Presidential Decree No. 1767 of October 27, 1993 ("On Regulation of Land Relations and Development of Agrarian Reform in Russia"), since the Land Code originally passed in April 1991, before the dissolution of the Soviet Union, has largely been invalidated by subsequent piece-meal legislation. The October 1993 presidential decree is supportive of the development of land markets in that it gives owners the right to sell, bequeath, mortgage, rent, and exchange land. A recent presidential decree of March 7, 1996 (entitled "On Realization of the Constitutional Rights of Citizens Concerning Land") reaffirms individual property rights by allowing practically all transactions in land shares and by removing restrictions on the amount of land that can be leased for farming. Removal of restrictions on leasing is an important positive development. Experience in East Central Europe, where land markets have been functioning for several years, indicates that leasing is much more prevalent than purchase and sale of land. Active rental markets in land provide flexibility for transfer, and allow owners to observe land values. The recent presidential decree is therefore a positive step, but legislative mechanism based on presidential decrees is fragile, because decrees retain force only until passage of a new land code.

The Constitution and the Civil Code leave a number of issues open for detailed specification in subsequent legislation, and several laws that will affect land issues are currently under consideration. A draft of a new Land Code proposed by the traditionally conservative agrarian faction in the Russian Duma passed its first reading in June 1995, but failed to pass the second reading in November 1995. Its final adoption in the present version is in question because its provisions are in direct contradiction to the spirit of laws and presidential decrees that have governed land relations in Russia since 1991. It would furthermore require annulment of important existing legislation (the 1990 Law on Land Reform and significant portions of the 1990 Law on Peasant Farms). The tabling of this draft, however, is a reflection of the intense debate that surrounds questions of land ownership and agricultural reform in Russia, a debate that will probably continue with increased intensity in the new Duma in 1996.

The new Land Code, if adopted in its current version, would preclude the normal functioning of land markets by preventing free transfer of land to most efficient producers. The effect of this distortion would be to freeze the farming sector in its present inefficient structure and depress land values, ultimately acting against the interests of land owners, most of whom are currently share-holders in agricultural enterprises.

An important step in late 1995 was the adoption of the Law on Agricultural Cooperation, which came into effect in December 1995, replacing the outdated 1988 Soviet Law on Cooperation in the USSR. Some provisions of the new law on agricultural cooperatives are significantly less restrictive than the provisions of the draft Land Code. For example, the cooperative law allows members to lease their land shares to the cooperative while retaining ownership, an option not available in the draft Land Code. Pending laws of importance include a draft water code and a draft law "On Mortgage of Agricultural Land." The latter will be automatically rendered invalid if the draft Land Code is passed in its current version, since mortgage of agricultural land is explicitly prohibited in the draft.

Land Ownership

The Constitution recognizes that "land and other natural resources may be in private, state, and other forms of ownership" (article 9). It further affirms the right of "citizens and their associations" (i.e., both individuals and legal persons) to hold land in private ownership (article 36). Owners are granted rights freely to use and decide on disposition of land as long as use or disposition do not harm the environment or infringe on rights and legal interests of other parties. Conditions and means for land use and disposition are to be specified on the basis of federal law; that is, the Land Code. The Civil Code recognizes three forms of ownership: private, municipal, and state. It affirms the right of citizens and legal persons to own land, freely to use land, and to engage in transactions in land. The Civil Code specifies that land not owned by citizens, legal persons, or municipalities will be owned by the state.

Although the Constitution sanctions private ownership of land, ten constituent republics of the Russian Federation do not recognize private ownership of land within their territories (Tatarstan, Bashkiriya, Dagestan, Komi, Mariel, Kabardino-Balkariya, North Osetiya, Tuva, Yakutiya-Sakha, and Koryakiya). These republics base their position on article 72 of the Constitution, which affirms that questions regarding ownership, use, and disposition of land, mineral deposits, water and other natural resources will be decided jointly by the Russian Federation and the constituent republics. Article 72 reflects and perpetuates ambiguity regarding the jurisdiction of federal and regional authority in land issues. The new draft Land Code reaffirms the right of the constituent republics to decide independently on the assignment of land to different forms of ownership on their respective territories, in line with local custom and in compliance with the general principles of federal law.

In addition to private ownership of land by individuals and legal persons, the Civil Code recognizes other forms of land tenure, which are a carry-over from the Soviet regime, when private property was not allowed. These are lifetime inheritable possession and permanent or temporary use rights, which may be granted only in lands owned by the state or the municipalities. The freedom of disposition becomes progressively more restricted as the form of tenure changes from private ownership to use rights (Table 2.1).

Agricultural land in Russia has been largely privatized since 1992, i.e., transferred from the state sector to private ownership. The state now owns less than 17% of agricultural land (see Table 1.1 in Chapter 1). However, only 12% is individually owned: this is the land in private farms and subsidiary household plots. Most of the privatized land is in the status of joint ownership (*obshchaya sobstvennost'*) in collective enterprises that have recently reorganized as various partnerships, cooperatives, and shareholder structures. Joint, as opposed to individual, ownership is defined in the Civil Code as private ownership by two or more individuals. A characteristic feature of jointly owned property is that its disposition requires unanimous agreement of all co-owners. Joint ownership may be of two varieties: shared joint ownership (*dolevaya obshchaya sobstvennost'*), when individual shares in the jointly owned property are defined (without physical designation of the underlying asset, however), and undivided joint ownership (*sovmestnaya obshchaya sobstvennost'*), when individual shares are not defined. In the 1994 farm survey undertaken for this report, farm enterprise managers reported that 90% of their land was in shared joint ownership.

Between 1992 and 1995, when recipients of land shares in former collective farms assigned them to shareholding enterprises with the objective of continuing collective production (possibly only in the interim period), the precise legal status of joint ownership was unclear. The rights and obligations of the individual holder of a land share and the collective of shareholders were ambiguous. For example, it was not clear if title to the land would pass to the enterprise, nor was it clear if withdrawal of land by individual shareholders would require permission of all co-owners. Clarification of the status of jointly owned land in shareholding enterprises came with passage of the Civil Code in October 1994 and Government Resolution No. 96 ("On Procedure for Realization of Rights of Owners of Land and Asset Shares") in February 1995, after most shareholders had already assigned their land into joint ownership.

Table 2.1. Forms of Land Tenure and Associated Disposition Rights in the Russian Civil Code (October 1994)

Form of land tenure	Tenure holder	Source of land	Disposition rights
Private ownership (*chastnaya sobstvennost'*)	Individuals, legal persons	Private owners, municipalities, the state	Sell, give away as a gift, mortgage, lease out, any other legal use
Lifetime inheritable possession (*pozhiznennoye nasleduyemoye vladeniye*)	Individuals	Municipalities and the state	Lease out, allow temporary use without payment; buildings erected on land become private property
Permanent use rights (*postoyannoye pol'zovaniye*)	Individuals, legal persons	Municipalities and the state	Lease out or allow temporary use without payment with owner's permission only; buildings erected on land become private property
Temporary use rights (*vremennoye pol'zovaniye*)	Individuals, legal persons	Municipalities, the state, other use-right holders	None
Leasing (*arenda*)	Individuals, legal persons	Private owners, municipalities, the state, other use-right holders	None; subleasing of farm land usually not allowed

The Civil Code, in line with the accepted practice of property rights of business organizations in most developed countries, unambiguously states that any property invested by an individual upon entry into a business organization (whether a limited or unlimited liability partnership, a joint-stock company, or a producer cooperative) becomes the property of that organization and is no longer owned by the individual. Government Resolution No. 96 applies this principle to investment of land and asset shares by former collective farm members in a new agricultural enterprise. Thus, when individuals assign their land and asset shares to an agricultural enterprise in the form of statutory payment for the right to participate in the enterprise (as a contribution to the equity capital of the enterprise), the land and assets are transferred from the status of joint ownership by a group of individuals to the status of ownership by a corporation (an enterprise). Both are forms of private ownership, but the designation of the owner is totally different; in the one case the owner is the individual, and in the other the enterprise.

Under Government Resolution No. 96 the individual owner of a land share may lease out the land share to the enterprise (or to other individuals) or simply invest the use right of the land share in the enterprise instead of investing the land share itself. In these cases, the individual retains ownership of the land share and of the underlying asset. The by-laws of the enterprise determine whether investment of use rights is an option for potential investors in a given farm enterprise. The right of leasing land shares to the farm enterprise is now reaffirmed in the December 1995 Law on Agricultural Cooperation and in the March 1996 presidential decree.

The draft Land Code currently before the Russian Duma does not recognize the right of individuals to lease out their land share or invest the use right of the land share in the enterprise in order to retain ownership. Instead, the shareholder would be obliged to follow one of two courses: either invest the land share in a reorganizing enterprise, thus exchanging the land share for a share of stock in the enterprise and forfeiting land ownership, or exercise immediately the right of exit from the enterprise with a physical plot of land for individual farming.

Both the Civil Code and the draft Land Code retain, in addition to ownership, the traditional forms of land tenure, such as lifetime inheritable possession, permanent and temporary use right, and leasehold. Throughout the legal discussion in 1993 and 1994, lifetime inheritable possession and permanent use rights were viewed as transitional forms of tenure to be superseded by ownership, although land remained in these tenure forms pending reclassification. Under the 1991 Law on Peasant Farms, individual farmers began to receive land from the state in private ownership. The October 1993 Presidential Decree (No. 1767) allowed people holding land under lifetime inheritable possession, permanent use right, and leasehold from the state to convert their tenure to ownership in accordance with existing legal procedures, such as restrictions on maximum holdings. The transitional forms of tenure were expected to diminish naturally as conversion proceeded. The draft Land Code, on the contrary, would abolish further allocation of land in private ownership to new farmers and thus re-emphasize anachronistic forms of land tenure, such as permanent use right of state-owned land.

The Civil Code and other early legislation contain some legal principles that may constitute a serious obstacle to security of ownership and tenure. Land is subject to a number of obligations, which pertain to agricultural land in all forms of tenure, including private ownership. Among these are the obligation to use land for its specified purpose, i.e., for farming, and the obligation to preserve the fertility of the land. Failure to fulfill these obligations can lead to administrative termination of tenure rights. An individual or an enterprise may lose rights to farm land if the land is allowed to remain uncultivated or to be used other than for farming. This provision applies even to privately owned land, which may be taken away from the delinquent owner despite legal title. These restrictions, which are retained in the present draft of the new Land Code, unduly constrain changes in land use, many of which in any event will be consistent with rational use of land. The provisions furthermore create opportunities for administrative interference and corruption.

Land Transactions

The Constitution and the Civil Code protect the right of land owners to decide on disposition of their land subject to provisions of the relevant federal legislation. Because the Constitution is worded to protect only general rights of ownership and disposition, and defers to federal law with regard to constraints on transactions, the highest piece of federal legislation with regard to land; i.e., the Land Code, will determine whether land owners have broad or narrow rights to conduct transactions in land. The status of the federal land code in relation to local land law, as well as its content, will need clarification in order for rights to engage in land transactions to be fully specified. A land code specifying broad powers of transaction will expedite development of land markets, and hence facilitate transfer of land to most efficient producers, improve land values, and increase investment in agriculture. The federal land code should explicitly protect rights to rent, sell, and mortgage land, so that provincial and local authorities cannot impose restrictions on transactions. Because of the very general wording of the Constitution with regard to land transactions, the federal land code is the key legal instrument through which rights to engage in land transactions can be affirmed.

The basis for land transactions is provided at present by presidential decrees of October 27, 1993, "On Regulation of Land Relations and Development of Agrarian Reform," and March 7, 1996, "On

Realization of the Constitutional Rights of Citizens Concerning Land." These decrees largely superseded the provisions of the old April 1991 Land Code, and their main purpose was to establish the legal status of land shares within agricultural enterprises. A second purpose was to sanction the right to conduct transactions in land. According to the decrees of October 1993 and March 1996, land owners have the right to sell, bequeath, mortgage, rent, and exchange land. Land owners also may exercise land rights by leasing their land out to private farmers or assigning it to various forms of shareholding enterprises. The March 1996 decree removes restrictions on the amount of land that can be leased in or out for farming.

The presidential decrees and the Civil Code provide relatively full assurance of the right to lease land in and out. This right applies to privately owned land, as well as land held in lifetime inheritable possession and in use right (see Table 2.1). During the early stage of development of land markets in Russia, rental transactions will be important. Energetic farm operators may desire to rent land from pensioners (who constitute nearly half the holders of land shares) and other owners or from the state and thus increase the efficiency of land use even if the operators are not in a position to buy additional land.

The draft Land Code in general reaffirms the right to rental transactions, and in fact introduces the option of long-term leasing. Individuals who lease from the state or from enterprises would hold leases of up to 50 years, with a preemptive right to renew the lease. Lease rights, with the preemptive option, would be inheritable. The draft Land Code does not set a specific upper limit to the area of land that can be rented in, although it stipulates that farm enterprises are allowed to lease out land to private farmers "up to an optimal size." It is desirable that leasing not be constrained by size limits in order to facilitate rational use of land. This position has indeed been adopted in the March 1996 presidential decree, and unconstrained rental transactions should be affirmed in the future Land Code.

The draft Land Code, contrary to the provisions of the March 1996 presidential decree, would limit rental rights of private farmers. Individual private farmers, in contrast to farm enterprises, would be allowed under the draft Land Code to rent out to other users not more than half of their land and only for a term of five years, except in case of retirement and certain special circumstances (disability of the farm operator, election to an official duty, service in the armed forces, full time student status). The wording of the restrictions provides scope for many exceptions, but could still constrain rental markets. For example, in market economies much agricultural land is owned by people over the age of 55 who choose to rent their land to younger operators even though they are still able-bodied. As the pension age is raised in Russia from its current level (55 for women, 62 for men), a large number of middle aged and elderly land owners may be prevented from renting out their land because they do not qualify yet for pension. Farm enterprises would also be prohibited from renting out more than 50% of their holdings. These provisions of the law are most likely intended to prevent creation of a rentier class of owners who do not operate their farms. As an alternative approach to preventing absentee ownership, local authorities could specify different tax rates to be paid by the land owner for farm land that is operated by the owner's family and for farm land rented out. The draft Land Code indeed proposes differential taxation in order to prevent speculative land sales after a short holding period (less than 5 years), and the same market mechanism instead of arbitrary administrative measures could be legitimately used also for other purposes. In general it is desirable that land owners be free to choose, without external constraints, the portion of their land that they work themselves, and the portion they rent in or out.

The draft Land Code furthermore would eliminate pensioners' option to rent land out. Pensioners are the segment of the population for whom the option of leasing out land may be essential for maintaining a reasonable standard of living. According to the current version of the draft, the pensioners would only be able to invest their land shares in a farm enterprise. The pensioners would thus forfeit ownership and lock themselves into a single shareholding structure, without the freedom to choose who would actually pay them for cultivating their land. This provision of the draft Land Code is completely at variance with the March 1996 presidential decree, which specifically allows pensioners to lease out or assign their land shares to producers in return for a lifetime annuity.

In addition to restrictions on leasing of land, the draft Land Code would practically eliminate the purchase of farm land from other than state sources and the sale of farm land among individuals and agricultural enterprises. Only the land in subsidiary household plots (the portion up to 0.5 ha around the house) and in small vegetable gardens and livestock associations could be sold at any time (subject to the standard restriction on use). The privatized land of farm enterprises could not be sold: it could be leased out, but only up to 50% of the holdings. Surplus privatized land would have to be returned to the state. Individual farmers who received land in private ownership prior to the proposed law would not be allowed to sell it: land could be alienated only to the state. For new private farmers created after the passage of the new law, the problem of selling land would not arise: they would receive land in lifetime inheritable possession, without the right to sell, and would be allowed to obtain additional land by purchasing from the state (or by leasing from the state, from farm enterprises, or from other private farmers).

The current draft of the Land Code appears to be in substantial contradiction to the provisions of previous presidential decrees, which promoted relative freedom of transactions in land. This point is forcefully made in the explanatory notes to the draft law, where it is argued that the presidential decrees ignore constitutional provisions and local custom in the Russian Federation. The new Land Code, if it were to be adopted in its present form, would eliminate much of the progress toward market-oriented land relations that has been achieved since 1991.

Mortgage of Land

Under current Russian law (October 1993 Presidential Decree No. 1767 and the Civil Code) land owners have the right to mortgage land. Land held in other forms of tenure may not be mortgaged by the holder. Banks, however, do not yet in prac-

tice accept land as collateral, and most loans that are secured with assets are secured with machinery, equipment, or animals. In order for mortgage financing to develop normally, land markets must be active enough to yield observable market values for land, since it is the market value that determines the collateral value of a parcel of land. So far, valuation of land in Russia is based on "normative tables" calculated using administratively prescribed formulas, which are not directly related to real economic values.

The elements of the draft Land Code that effectively preclude development of land markets also preclude development of mortgage financing. In addition, however, the current draft explicitly prohibits mortgage of agricultural land, and thus eliminates an important source of investment financing not only for small farmers but also for farm enterprises.

Farm Restructuring

The initial impetus for farm restructuring derived from presidential decree "On Immediate Measures for Implementation of Land Reform" of December 27, 1991, and government resolution "On Procedures for Reorganizing State and Collective Farms" of December 29, 1991. These documents defined a process whereby within approximately one year the farms would call general assemblies to vote on reorganization, and thereafter register according to the decision of the meeting; i.e., either under the same form of organization, or under the newly chosen form. Upon registration the farm would assume ownership of its land in the name of the shareholders, unless the assembly elected to remain a state farm. Non-land assets were already owned by the shareholders if the farm was in the past a collective farm, but upon reorganization the ownership would be made explicit through the designation and distribution of shares. Shareholders of newly reorganized state farms received share ownership of non-land assets upon registry as one of the non-state forms of organization. As shown in Table 1.2 in Chapter 1, 95% of farms had gone through the process by 1994. Nearly half of farm enterprises registered as closed shareholding farms, both joint stock companies and limited liability partnerships, and 35% of farms elected to remain collective or state farms.

The December 1991 government resolution defined the general outlines of the share system. The resolution did not offer guidance for farms that wished to proceed beyond creation of a shareholding structure essentially the same as the predecessor state or collective farm. Nor did this resolution require that farms determine the value of individual asset shares and the size and location of individual land shares, or distribute share documents to shareholders. Although compliance with the announced regulations was high, it was largely formal. Many farm employees surveyed in the winter of 1992-1993 were not aware that their farms had changed organizational form (Brooks and Lerman, 1994). In 1992 few farms determined land and asset shares, and even fewer distributed entitlement documents to shareholders. Additional instructions on determination of land and asset shares were issued in a government resolution of September 4, 1992. By early 1994, 90% of managers in the sample used for this study indicated that the size and value of shares had been determined on paper. Few farms had distributed assets corresponding to the shares, and few farms began paying dividends to shareholders. The share determination did not have much practical value other than as a step toward future restructuring, but this step had been taken on most farms by the end of 1993.

Where members chose to implement a more fundamental internal restructuring, a methodology was needed to match actual land and physical assets to shares, and to allow regrouping and trading of shares to form new business units in place of the original shareholding farm. A number of farms proceeded on their own initiative, but in the absence of more detailed guidelines, practical issues of implementation limited the process. A methodology for designing and conducting an internal "auction" (a "redistribution meeting") for land and physical assets against shares was pioneered on a small number of pilot farms in Nizhnii Novgorod Province in 1992 and 1993, and implemented more widely in several provinces in 1994 and 1995. The Nizhnii Novgorod experience received formal

acknowledgment and recognition in two Government resolutions: "On the Practice of Agrarian Transformation in Nizhnii Novgorod Province" (April 1994) and "On Agricultural Enterprise Reform Allowing for the Experience in Nizhnii Novgorod Province" (July 1994). These resolutions recommended that the principles used for farms in Nizhnii Novgorod Province be extended to all of Russia. A summary of the Nizhnii Novgorod farm restructuring procedure is presented in Table 2.2.

Table 2.2. Nizhnii Novgorod Farm Restructuring Procedure

Preparatory Work
o   Inventory of land and assets
o   Preparation of eligibility lists
o   Calculation of land and asset shares
o   Approval of distribution plan by General Assembly

Stage 1: Distribution of Shares
o   Distribution of share certificates to eligible individuals
o   Acquainting shareholders with their rights and options

Stage 2: Creating New Enterprises
o   Identification of technologically independent subdivisions of existing farm
o   Regrouping of shareholders through negotiation, registration of enterprises
o   Concluding contracts between shareholders joining the various enterprises

Stage 3: Auctions
o   Division of land and assets into lots
o   Submission of bids for land and asset lots
o   Physical distribution of land and assets through an auction

Stage 4: Transfer of Property Rights
o   Physical transfer of land and assets
o   Issuance of title

With the exception of the farms that were wholly reorganized through the Nizhnii Novgorod pilot program and its recent extension, most reorganizations did not proceed beyond re-registration of the original farm under a new form. The differences among the various new organizational forms were not clearly specified legally, nor perceived by participants, and the choice of form appeared to be arbitrary.

One of the main lessons of the Nizhnii Novgorod project was that participants needed close guidance and intensive advice in order to move beyond formal re-registration to actual restructuring. By early 1995, the pace of farm restructuring appeared to have stalled at the stage of formal registration with little substantive change. Government Resolution No. 96 of February 1, 1995, was intended to strengthen the legal basis for transactions in land and asset shares and further clarify procedures for reorganization for farms that had not yet reorganized. The provisions of Resolution No. 96 with regard to land remain in effect until passage of the new Land Code. In addition to clarifying transactions with shares, the resolution provides sample documents for recording transactions in land and shares.

Some enterprises (1900 nationwide) registered as agricultural producers' cooperatives between 1992 and 1995. This form of organization was among the options specified in the decrees and it is one of the business structures recognized by the Civil Code. However, the legal structure of producer cooperatives was not well defined due to lack of a cooperative law. A new Law on Agricultural Cooperation was adopted in December 1995. The law recognizes agricultural production cooperatives and a wide range of service cooperatives that may engage in processing, marketing, input supply, farm and rural services, and even credit and insurance. Production cooperatives are based on member labor, which may be augmented with hired workers. Service cooperatives, on the other hand, do not require members to work in the cooperative: the only requirement is that members take part in the business activity of the service cooperative.

An agricultural enterprise currently registered under other forms of organization can follow the procedures of the Civil Code and the Law on Agricultural Cooperation to reorganize and register as a production cooperative. The new cooperative law contains fairly detailed provisions on creation of cooperatives in the process of restructuring of agricultural organizations. In practice, it is expected that all remaining *kolkhozes* and a number of other shareholding and limited liability structures will reorganize and register as agricultural production cooperatives. The term "collective," the root word of *kolkhoz*, will no longer be used to describe these agricultural enterprises, which will instead be cooperative farms, or *koopkhozy*. The new law of

cooperatives is likely to bring a large share of agricultural resources under its jurisdiction.

The Ambiguous Status of Land Shares

Land shares are created and defined when a state or collective farm begins the process of conversion to a privatized shareholding enterprise. The preamble to the December 1991 resolution on farm restructuring states that shareholders have an unconditional right to remove land and asset shares from an agricultural enterprise in order to start a private farm, without receiving permission of the farm administration or the general assembly of the members. According to the government resolutions of 1991 and 1992, recipients of land shares are required to file an intention of disposition of the share with the internal farm commission for reorganization. The options for disposition of land shares include: receipt of land and/or other assets in physical form upon exit to start a private farm or other activity outside the enterprise; sale of the share to other members or to the enterprise; investment of the share in the equity capital of an agricultural enterprise, which is broadly defined to include the former collective or state farm in its new form, as well as a variety of other legal forms of organization, such as partnerships, joint-stock societies, or producer cooperatives.

If a shareholder withdraws land and starts a private farm in combination with others, the land is registered as joint property of all farm owners. The land can be reclaimed by the individual only if the private farm is dissolved. Agreement of all co-owners is required to sell a portion of the land.

Treatment of Land Shares in Government Resolution No. 96 of February 1995

The 1991-1992 government resolutions do not specify what happens to the land share if it is not withdrawn for private farming, and is instead invested in establishment of a new agricultural enterprise. Government Resolution No. 96 of February 1995 clarifies the ambiguity on the basis of the 1994 Civil Code by stating that if the shareholder invests the land share in the equity capital of an agricultural enterprise, the enterprise assumes ownership of a land plot corresponding in size to that of the land share, and the shareholder loses ownership rights to the land. As a result, the shareholder also loses the right to request allocation of a physical plot upon exit. However, instead of investing the land share in an agricultural enterprise, the individual has the option according to Resolution No. 96 to lease the share to the enterprise for a short term or to invest the use right of the land share in the enterprise for a period not exceeding three years. In either case, the individual retains ownership of the land share and can subsequently (upon termination of the agreed term) request to withdraw land in kind and exit from the enterprise to establish a private farm.

While Resolution No. 96 establishes a procedure only for exit of owners of land shares (i.e., individuals who have not invested their shares in the equity capital of an agricultural enterprise), the Civil Code provides guidelines also for the more general case of exit of any individual from an enterprise. Upon exit from an enterprise of any organizational form except a joint-stock company, the individual receives the value of the share of the investment in the enterprise. The value can be received in cash or in kind (land or assets in physical form). In limited liability partnerships and societies, compensation in kind has to be negotiated with the other owners of the enterprise. In producer cooperatives, the choice between the two options is left to the cooperative charter. In joint-stock companies, the exiting individual simply has to find a buyer for the stock, as is the standard practice everywhere in the world.

Treatment of Land Shares in Recent Legislation: December 1995 Cooperative Law and March 1996 Presidential Decree

The Law on Agricultural Cooperation of December 1995 specifies that a member entering a cooperative can use the privately owned land plot or the land share as the initial statutory investment in the equity capital of the cooperative. In this event, the land plot or the land share become the property of the cooperative. Alternatively, the member can lease the land plot to the cooperative,

retaining ownership. This provision of the new cooperative law is clearly at variance with the current draft of the Land Code, which only allows partial and short-term leasing of privately owned plots. In order to take advantage of the legal right to retain ownership of their land share, prospective members must be able to meet the investment requirement in the equity capital of the cooperative from other resources. Since few prospective members have capital other than land and asset shares in the former farm enterprise, membership in a producer cooperative will involve transfer of land ownership to the cooperative in many cases.

The cooperative law, similarly to the Civil Code, provides that upon exit members receive the value of their share in the cooperative, either in cash or in kind. Exit with a physical plot of land in principle is not conditioned on the member's intention to establish a private farm. The decision between the two alternatives of cash redemption or allocation of a physical plot is left to the cooperative charter, or to the general assembly if the charter does not address the issue.

The new cooperative law was followed by a presidential decree of March 1996, which consolidated some of the principles of land reform that appeared threatened by the draft land code before the Duma. The decree provides a detailed list of what owners can do with land shares. This list gives land owners the right to engage practically in any transaction in land shares, as long as the use of land for farming is protected. Moreover, transactions in land shares do no require consent of other shareholders in the organization. In addition to selling the land share, exchanging it for an asset share or another land share, passing in inheritance, or giving it as a gift, the owner may request conversion of the land share into a physical plot in order to establish an individual farm or lease the plot to another private farmer, household, or farm enterprise. The land share can be invested in the equity capital of a farm enterprise. Alternatively, if the holder of the land share decides to retain ownership of the share, its use right can be leased to an agricultural producer.

Treatment of Land Shares in Draft Land Code

The existing Land Code predates the whole concept of land shares, which have accordingly been treated so far in various decrees and resolutions. The draft of the new Land Code under consideration by the Duma devotes much space to land and asset shares. The draft states that the land share exists only during the period of reorganization of the enterprise. Recipients of land shares must decide during the reorganization either to withdraw land for the purpose of private farming or invest the land share in a new agricultural enterprise. The new agricultural enterprise is not necessarily identical with the physical extent of the original enterprise: the former enterprise may split into a number of smaller enterprises in the process of reorganization, and the individuals can choose which of the new structures to join. Upon investment in a new enterprise, however, the property right passes to the enterprise, and the land share loses its legal identity. In the December 1995 law of agricultural cooperatives, ownership of land likewise passes to the cooperative enterprise when the land shares are used to pay for the membership share in the equity capital of the cooperative. In both cases, these provisions for transfer of ownership are consistent with the principles of the Civil Code. The draft Land Code, however, does not include the option of the February 1995 Government Resolution No. 96 and the December 1995 cooperative law, which allow leasing of land shares and investment of use rights of land shares without foregoing ownership.

The draft Land Code, similarly to the Civil Code, also provides a limited mechanism for exit of individuals after the establishment of the enterprise, when individually owned land shares have effectively ceased to exist. The draft Land Code states that individuals have a right to exit with a plot of land "by agreement with the enterprise" for the purpose of establishing a private farm. If the parties fail to reach an agreement, the matter is referred to local agricultural authorities or the courts, which may grant the individual a plot of land if that individual originally invested a land share in the enterprise and is legally entitled to be a private farmer. The same article, however, stipulates that a plot of land will be granted to the exiting individual

if this "does not cause damage to the economic well-being of the agricultural enterprise and the profitability of production, unless the exiting member undertakes to compensate the agricultural enterprise for the ensuing damage, including loss of income." Perhaps in an attempt to offset the impact of this seemingly draconian clause, the draft Land Code includes another affirmative condition, which states that a plot of land will be granted if "the land in the enterprise or part of the land is used inefficiently (the yield is 50% or less of the district average for land of comparable quality)..." Individuals who wish to exit for purposes other than private farming have to work for 10 years in the reorganized enterprise until they become eligible to receive the value of their land share or, by special agreement, a physical plot of land.

All these conditionalities may present serious obstacles to the exit of individuals with land from enterprises after the initial stage of reorganization. A recent commentary in the Russian newspaper *Izvestiya* indeed asserts that the draft Land Code encourages creation of large latifundias in place of existing giant collectives (Uzun, 1995). In reality, the outcome of the ongoing debate around land reform and land ownership will depend on the language of the final laws, the public and political atmosphere, and ultimately on the interpretation adopted by the courts.

Outcomes and Next Steps

The legal developments in 1995 address a fundamental ambiguity with regard to land shares. Land cannot simultaneously be owned by individual shareholders and by the enterprises with which they are associated. Actual legislation of 1995 (Government Resolution No. 96 and the Law on Agricultural Cooperation) and the draft Land Code recognize the property right of the enterprise unless an individual chooses to leave the enterprise or makes special arrangements to retain ownership. By strengthening the tenure rights of shareholding enterprises, current and pending legislation implies a strong tendency toward corporatization of Russian agriculture. Corporatization is evident in the units created during the formal reorganization from 1992 to 1995, and in those emerging from whole-farm reorganizations according to the Nizhnii Novgorod model. The observed tendency toward the creation of large-scale corporate farms, rather than smaller or mid-size family farms, is not consistent with the observed practice in agriculture in developed countries, nor with the current relative factor costs in Russia, where labor is cheap and capital assets are expensive. This discrepancy suggests the need for continued restructuring of Russian farm enterprises.

Size Distribution of Reorganized Russian Farms

Farm size in a market economy is an economic variable that reflects many causative factors. Farm operators adjust farm size over time by buying and selling land, or renting land in or out to increase the economic return to the farming operation. The farm operator seeks a return to his or her labor at least equivalent to alternative jobs available through the labor market. The operator seeks a return to capital in the operation equivalent to the risk-adjusted return to alternative financial assets. Where capital is expensive relative to labor, the operator will tend to substitute labor for capital, and use labor intensive production techniques. Yet in agriculture the cost of supervising a number of hired workers dispersed over a large area tends to be high. Costs of supervision explain the high frequency of family farms with family labor supplemented by a few hired workers in many market economies. Thus where labor is cheap and capital expensive, farms will on average tend to be small. Where labor is expensive farm size will tend to be larger, except in cases such as the European Union, where high producer support prices raise the price of land and reduce farm size much below that of North America. Size varies according to the predominant kind of activity on the farm, but analysis of the relationship between farm size and productivity has shown that farms so large that a family cannot provide most of the labor and management are not more efficient than mid-sized family operations. Only in plantation crops, such as bananas, is there a clear apparent advantage to large size, and the advantage derives largely from the need to process the product rapidly after harvest (Binswanger, Deininger, and

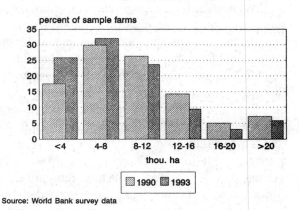

Fig. 2.1. Size Distribution of Farm Enterprises Russia 1990-1993

Source: World Bank survey data

Feder, 1995).

In the Russian economy in the 1990s labor is inexpensive relative to capital, and the quantity of labor available for agricultural work is likely to increase for a period, as adjustment in the industrial sector proceeds. Economic factors can thus be expected to create a tendency for small farms to have lower costs than large farms. Yet the inherited capital stock favors large scale production, and independent small scale operators are not yet well served by market services. Farm enterprises included in the sample for this study are very large by world standards. Although they declined in size between 1990 and 1993 by approximately 15%, largely through transfer of land to the redistribution fund and through augmentation of household plots of members, the average farm size remained at about 8000 ha. Approximately 25% of enterprises were 4000 ha or smaller in 1993, compared to approximately 17% in 1990 (Fig. 2.1).

As the inherited capital stock is retired and market services improve, more agricultural producers are likely to judge that small and mid-sized family operations would yield them a superior return to their land and asset shares. The farm size preferred by farm operators will probably be much smaller than the initial size of the shareholding farms created to date. Shareholders will wish to withdraw shares and reconfigure the very large farms. Some amendment in the legal framework to facilitate exit and reconfiguration will be needed to give adequate flexibility to Russian farm structure as it responds to the new economic environment.

When a farm undergoes reorganization through the internal auction process (the Nizhnii Novgorod model), the new enterprises created are smaller than the original farm, but still large by world standards. Fig. 2.2 shows the outcome of reorganization through auction in spring of 1995 in Rostov, Orel, and Ryazan provinces. Here, 10 traditional farms ranging in size from less than 2000 ha to 20,000 ha reorganized into 46 new enterprises, 19 of which were private farms and 27 other types of farms. The average private farm had 49 ha after reorganization. Among farms of other types, 70% exceeded 1000 ha. Nevertheless, the process of farm reorganization in these three provinces is characterized by significant downsizing: the median farm among those larger than 1000 ha represented less than 1/3 of the size of the old farm before reorganization.

Figure 2.3 shows the size distribution of units created through the auction process in Nizhnii Novgorod Province. A total of six large-scale farms were reorganized, with initial average size of over 3000 ha (ranging in size from 1640 ha to 3871 ha). The reorganization produced 52 new farms, with average size of just under 350 ha and median size of 84 ha. Among the new farms, 56% are smaller than 100 ha and 20% are smaller than 20 ha. At the other extreme, 20% of the new farms are larger than 500 ha and 10% larger than 1000 ha.

In contrast to the present structure of Russian farm enterprises, only about 3% of American farms are larger than 840 ha, or 2000 acres (Fig. 2.4). Conditions in labor and capital markets in America are more likely to produce large farms than is the case in Russia, since labor in America is expensive relative to capital, and wages outside agriculture are high. Nonetheless, there are few farms as large as what would be considered a small enterprise in traditional Russian agriculture.

Exit: The Need for a Mechanism

The current program of land reform and farm restructuring in Russia is based on the principles of democracy and informed voluntarism. Participants in the process receive shares and have access to information about alternative ways in which to us e

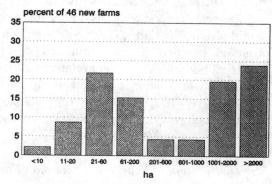

Fig. 2.2. Size Distribution of New Farms Orel, Rostov, Ryazan Provinces

Source: IFC

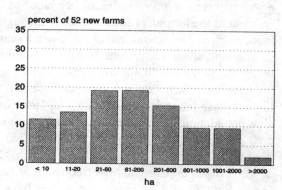

Fig. 2.3. Size Distribution of New Farms Nizhnii Novgorod Province

Source: IFC

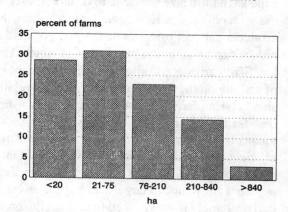

Fig. 2.4. Size Distribution of US Farms

Source: USDA, 1987 farm census

their shares. The farm structure that has developed reflects the voluntary decisions made by participants with the information they commanded at the time they made their decisions, and in the sectoral environment in which the decisions were made. The sectoral environment will continue to change as markets develop and the gaps between producer prices and border prices narrow. People who received asset shares will have a changing understanding of how best to use their assets.

The present legal environment offers little protection to individuals or small groups who seek to exit with land and assets from enterprises that are neither bankrupt nor in the process of full restructuring. The land code or separate legislation of equivalent stature should protect the rights of holders of land shares to withdraw land in kind, either as individuals or in small groups, from shareholding enterprises. Once the right to exit is protected, a mechanism should be designed to operationalize this right.

Under one possible mechanism, the exiting individuals could propose a parcel of land and other assets that they would accept in redemption of their shares. If the enterprise and the exiters could agree on a match, then the transaction would take place and be legally registered. If no agreement could be reached in a specified time period, then the entire enterprise would be legally required to undergo a new internal auction against shares of all members.

In the absence of this or a similar mechanism, people choosing to remain in farming but wishing to leave their original shareholding enterprise would not have access to land. Agricultural workers would have the option either to stay in the large units much like the prior collectives, or exit as landless laborers with some monetary compensation. Under these circumstances the sector would sacrifice the flexibility of structure needed in order for Russian agriculture to increase in competitiveness. The restructuring procedure for agricultural corporations should thus be one that facilitates physical restructuring through withdrawal of physical assets, instead of simply sale of shares.

References to Chapter 2

H. Binswanger, K. Deininger, and G. Feder. 1995. "Power, Distortion, Revolt and Reform in Agricultural Land Relations," in: J. Behrman and T. N. Srinivasan, eds., *Handbook of Development Economics*, vol. III, ch. 42, pp. 2659-2772, Elsevier, New York.

K. Brooks and Z. Lerman. 1994. *Land Reform and Farm Restructuring in Russia*, World Bank Discussion Paper 233, The World Bank, Washington, D.C.

V. Uzun. 1995. "Private farming may be derailed by the new Land Code," *Finansovye Izvestiya*, No. 68 (197), September 26.

3. Reorganization of Large Farm Enterprises

The survey of managers of large farm enterprises in 1994 reveals a sector little changed since the 1992 survey. Farms are marginally smaller but still large by world standards, production has declined, farm finances have deteriorated, and pessimism about the future has deepened. Few farms have moved beyond the determination of shares to fundamental restructuring, and the changes in organization are essentially those observed in the 1992 survey. The reasons for this apparent stagnation in restructuring of large enterprises derive in part from deficiencies in the legal framework presented in Chapter 2, and in part from discriminatory sectoral policies discussed in Chapter 1. The following chapter presents a more detailed picture of the status of farm enterprises in early 1994.

The sample of farm managers in the 1994 survey covers 234 enterprises, of which prior to the reform (in 1990) 52% were collective farms (*kolkhozes*) and 43% state farms (*sovkhozes*). The remaining farms were originally interfarm enterprises or subsidiary farms of industrial entities.

Fully 92% of managers reported in the first quarter of 1994 that a decision to reorganize had been taken. This proportion is practically the same as in the winter 1992 survey, when already 90% of farm managers responded that their farms had discussed the reorganization issue and made a decision. The passing of a formal decision on reorganization is thus not an obstacle to restructuring of Russian farm enterprises.

The percentage of farms that have decided to reorganize is practically the same among collective and state farms. The most preferred form of new organization is a partnership (*tovarishchestvo*) or a collective enterprise (*kollektivnoye predpriyatiye*): half the respondents chose this form, which is formally very similar to the old collective farm (Table 3.1). One third of the respondents indicated that the farm had decided to reorganize as a closed joint-stock company, i.e., an organization in which

shares are available only to insiders and cannot be traded on open market. While sovkhozes split evenly between these two forms of organization, kolkhozes tended to reorganize as partnerships or collective enterprises (Table 3.1). As many as 6% of the farms that discussed reorganization decided to keep their old form (mostly a *kolkhoz*), although there were no legal provisions preventing change of organization. Only 2% among the *sovkhozes* chose to remain state farms, as this form naturally prevents them from assuming ownership of land and assets.

Table 3.1. Forms of Farm Reorganization (percent of respondents)

	All Farms	Former Kolkhozes	Former Sovkhozes
Not reorganized	8.1	6.6	7.0
Reorganized:			
Keep old form	5.6	9.1	2.0
Partnership/Collective enterprise	45.7	49.6	45.0
Join-stock society			
closed	30.3	20.7	41.0
open	0.5	--	--
Association of peasant farms	0.5	0.5	--
Farmers' cooperative	3.0	3.3	3.0
Division into several farms	2.6	5.0	--
Not yet decided/other	3.8	5.0	2.0
Number of farms	234	121	100

The average farm size in the sample declined by about 15% from 9500 ha in 1990 to 8000 ha in 1993. The farm size distribution shifted toward smaller farms in 1993, but the farms remain very large by world standards. Farms of 8000 ha or smaller represented nearly 60% of the sample in 1993, compared to 47% in 1990 (Fig. 3.1). Large farms appear to have lost a smaller percentage of their holdings than small farms (the correlation coefficient between percentage decrease and farm size in 1990 is negative). Despite modest changes in farm size, the overall structure of land holdings in farm enterprises did not change between 1990 and 1993. Arable land continued to account for 65% of land holdings, pasture and hayland for nearly 30%, and forests for around 6%.

Farms transferred land mainly to the district redistribution fund (47% of total transfer) and the village council (31%). These two authorities are designated by law as the source of land for private farmers and household plots, and transfer of land from farm enterprises is intended to create a sufficient land reserve for new individual users. Farm managers in the sample reported that they transferred land to private farmers (18% of total land transfers) and household plots (4%). It is not clear that these are indeed direct transfers from farm enterprises to private farmers and household plots, since farm managers may have double counted by reporting land transferred to individuals through the redistribution reserve. The average household plot in the sampled farms increased very modestly from 0.21 ha in 1992 to 0.29 ha in 1994.

State-owned land in the sample is 10% of all farmland (excluding forests), down from 100% prior to the reforms (Fig. 3.2). In this sense, agricultural land in Russia has been basically privatized, and 91% of respondents reported that their farms have a formal certificate of land ownership. Yet nearly 90% of the land in farm enterprises (excluding forests) is owned by collectives, and less than 0.5% is owned by individuals. Most of the collectively owned land is in shared ownership (80% of farmland excluding forests), with land shares assigned to individuals at least on paper. Less than 10% is joint or undivided ownership, the initial stage of land transfer from the state to the collective, before any share assignment has been made to individual members.

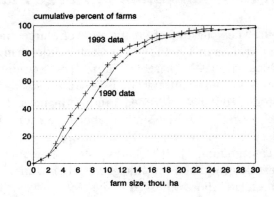

Fig. 3.1. Size Distribution of Farm Enterprises: 1990-1993

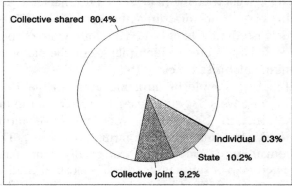

Fig. 3.2. Land Ownership in Farm Enterprises

Average farm size 8125 ha

Distribution of land and asset shares to individuals is the first step toward farm restructuring after formal registration as a new organizational form. Although share certificates in themselves do not produce any internal changes in farms, they create the conditions for reorganization and regrouping from within. Fully 90% of the farms in the sample have gone through the process of allocating individual share certificates in land and assets to their members. However, so far these are "conditional" shares, i.e., paper shares recorded in central bookkeeping: the land plots corresponding to the shares have not been marked out in the field, nor have assets been distributed in physical form.

The average size of a land share in the sample is 12.5 ha per person. Approximately 550 individuals per farm, including employees, pensioners, and social service workers, are entitled to land shares. On an average farm, the employees represent nearly 60% of recipients of land shares, the pensioners are around 30%, and workers of the social sphere are the remaining 10%. In all farms in the sample both employees and pensioners are eligible to receive land shares, which is consistent with existing legal provisions. Nearly 80% of farm assemblies in the sample used their legal discretion to allocate land shares to workers of the social sphere not directly employed by the farm enterprise, although they were not required by law to include these individuals.

Employees and pensioners also received shares in non-land assets on all farms that reorganized. Furthermore, 15% of farms calculated asset shares for former employees who left the enterprise before the distribution date, and 10% of farms assigned shares to other beneficiaries (presumably workers of the social sphere in the village). The calculation of the size of an asset share was based on length of tenure and salary, as stipulated by law and prevailing practice. Biases in the traditional wage structure, such as the high wages for drivers of tractors and vehicles, were thus reflected in the distribution of asset shares.

Most managers (over 70%) indicated that their non-land assets were privatized in 1992. The value of the individual asset share was estimated at 2.2 million rubles at prices prevailing in the first quarter of 1994, or around $1000. The average number of asset shares per farm was around 500, which is comparable to the average number of land shares per farm. Nearly 70% of farm assets have been distributed in the form of shares, while the remaining 30% remains indivisible. These are mainly social assets that will be transferred to the village council or will remain under collective management.

Table 3.2. Rights Associated with Land and Asset Shares: Frequency of Different Rights as Reported by Farm-Enterprise Managers*

Rights	Land Shares		Asset Shares	
	1992	1994	1992	1994
Get land/asset upon leaving to start private farm	66.5	85.0	66.9	80.8
Get land upon leaving to take another job	18.8	15.8	NA	NA
Use asset share to purchase home	NA	NA	41.1	32.1
Bequeath share to heirs within farm enterprise	62.7	80.8	67.3	80.8
Bequeath share to any heirs	33.1	39.7	32.7	38.9
Receive dividends from farm profits	57.7	71.4	76.2	89.7
Receive distribution in kind	48.1	74.4	NA	NA
Sell share to farm enterprise	32.7	41.9	58.1	60.7
Sell share to other farm employees	31.2	37.6	52.3	53.4
Sell share to any buyer	NA	6.4	11.5	6.4
Receive value of share upon retirement	24.2	26.1	21.8	41.5
Receive value of share if fired	19.6	23.9	43.1	43.2
Exchange land share for asset share	15.8	14.5	10.0	9.4
No rights provided by charter	11.5	4.3	NA	6.0

* Percent of managers (out of 260 respondents in 1992 and 234 respondents in 1994) indicating that the particular right was associated with land or asset shares in their farm enterprise.

The rights associated with land and asset shares in farm enterprises are shown in Table 3.2. More than 70% of managers reported that shareholders are entitled to receive dividends from farm profits, to pass their shares in inheritance within the farm, and to convert the shares to a plot of land and physical assets upon leaving the enterprise to establish a private farm. These reported rights are consistent with provisions of existing laws. A higher proportion (over 80%) of managers recognized these legal rights in the 1994 survey than in the 1992 survey (65%), only a year and a half earlier (see Table 3.2). Knowledge and understanding of the laws pertaining to farm restructuring appears to have spread among the rural population in the two years between samples. Ironically, just as understanding of the legal rights of shareholders appears to be growing, the rights themselves are under threat of curtailment in draft legislation, such as the draft Land Code and the draft Law on Cooperatives. Under the present draft legislation, the right of shareholders or members to exit with land and assets would be strictly limited, even if the exiters desired to set up private farms.

Few farm managers in the sample reported that shareholders could take their land when leaving the farm for another job (other than private farming), or could exchange land shares for asset shares and vice versa. The right to exchange shares is a prerequisite for efficient regrouping of land and assets within farm enterprises. Over 40% of farm managers reported that members could receive the value of their asset shares upon retirement or when fired. Only 25% reported that shareholders could receive the value of land shares upon retirement or termination. In practice, monetary redemption of the value of land shares would be difficult on a large scale, since neither enterprises nor individuals can collateralize loans with land.

Although most farms report that shareholders are entitled to receive dividends, only 40% of the farms in the sample have decided on the percentage of profit to be distributed. On farms where the decision has been made, the average dividend was 16% of profits and the median dividend was 10%.

There is little indication that the shares in land and assets distributed by fully 90% of the farms to their employees and pensioners are more than paper certificates of entitlement. The responses suggesting that land plots have been distributed to individuals or that land plots are worked individually are too few to be considered reliable. Thus, 13 out of 234 farm managers (6%) indicated that a few tens of hectares (out of 3000-5000 ha assigned to land shares in each farm) had been distributed in physical form to members, but in 8 out of these 13 cases the plots were reported to be worked collectively, and not individually. These farms are concentrated in two provinces (Rostov and Orel). One farm in Saratov Province stands out as an exceptional case: its manager reported that, out of 8600 ha in land shares, 1500 ha had been distributed to individuals and were worked individually. Only 10 of 234 farms in the sample reported that assets had been distributed in physical form to members (after the calculation of the shares) and 5 farms reported that members had received the cash value of their asset shares. In 13 farms asset shares were reportedly applied to purchase privatized housing. Most of these farms are in Novosibirsk and Saratov provinces.

Managers on 105 farms (45% of the sample) reported that some individuals received asset shares in physical form. The average number of these individuals was only 15 per farm (out of some 500 shareholders), and the median was even lower (6 individuals). In 16 farms (7%), some members were reported to have sold their asset shares. The number of sellers was typically fewer than 20 per farm, with a median of 5 and an average of 17. These cases occurred across all five provinces in the sample.

Exits of Employees During Reorganization

The laws enabling employees to leave their farm enterprise with a share of land and assets in order to establish a private farm have produced a modest flow of families out of large-scale farms. Over two-thirds of managers in the sample (160 respondents) reported that some employees left to become private farmers. On average, 10 private farms were created per large-scale farm enterprise, each run by 2 former employees, probably a husband and wife team). Another 10 farm managers reported establishment of various partnerships, small enterprises, cooperatives, and other independent entities by former employees. Some 1400 individuals left their farm enterprises to join these independent structures in addition to the 3400 individuals who moved to private farming (Table 3.3). This is nearly 4% of the total number of employees in the sampled farm enterprises.

Table 3.3. Exit of Employees During Reorganization of Farm Enterprises

Organization created by exiting members	Managers reporting exits*	Number of exiting employees	Number of entities established
Private farm	68.4%	3437	1603
Partnership or small enterprise	2.6%	1344	8
Coop	0.5%	10	1
Other	0.9%	44	5

*Percent of 234 respondents.

Fig. 3.3. Exit of Employees During Reorganization

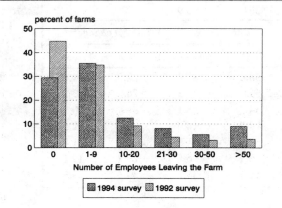

percent of farms

Number of Employees Leaving the Farm

1994 survey   1992 survey

Comparison of the number of employee exits during reorganization obtained in two consecutive surveys (1992 and 1994), indicates that the pace of exit accelerated slightly over the period, but remains quite low. Fully 50% of managers believe that the prospects for the development of private farming in their regions will diminish in the next 2-3 years. The proportion of farm managers reporting that no employees had left during reorganization dropped from 45% in 1992 to 30% in 1994 (Fig. 3.3). The proportion of farm enterprises in which more than 10 employees had left increased from 20% to 35%. While in 1992 the maximum number of employees exiting an enterprise was 134 and there was only one farm with more than 100 exits, the maximum number of exiting employees in early 1994 had risen to 850 in one instance and there were 9 farms with more than 100 exits (4% of the sample). Over 70% of farm managers in the five provinces reported that they sold farm services to private farmers in their region, thus offering further evidence that private farmers are a recognized presence, despite the widely noted failure of a number of private farms.

Attitudes toward Ownership of Land

Most managers in the survey (85%) support allocation of land for private farming, but many (65%) reported the opinion that land should be held in lifetime use or long-term lease from the state. Fewer than 20% of managers responding supported private ownership of land by private farmers. The attitude is different with regard to land in household plots: here 40% of managers support the right of families to own their household plots, although 55% prefer lifetime use or long-term leasing for this land as well. Among the managers favoring private ownership of land in household plots, fewer than half (43%) are of the opinion that private farmers should be allowed to own their land. Employees reported similar attitudes to private ownership of land: nearly 40% supported private ownership of household plots, and fewer than 20% supported private ownership of land allocated to private farmers. Both managers and employees thus perceive a qualitative difference between land in household plots and land in private farms: private ownership of household plots is more readily accepted than private ownership of commercial farm land.

Some 80% of farm managers expressed a negative view of the option to allow buying and selling of land in Russia. Nearly two-thirds of respondents who favored private land ownership for farmers and households did not favor legalized purchase and sale of land. Managers thus reported more acceptance of formal changes in land ownership than acceptance of market transactions in land. Managers' opinions regarding land markets are roughly consistent with those of employees surveyed, although employees are slightly more supportive of land markets. Among employees, two-thirds reported a negative attitude toward the decision to allow purchase and sale of commercial farm land in Russia, compared to four-fifths of managers. Among private farmers, more than half

supported market transactions in land, but curiously nearly 30% were opposed to buying and selling of land. On the whole, it appears that many people in rural Russia do not consider marketability as a necessary attribute of private ownership of land.

Organization and Changes in Farm Management

The managers in 1994 were more pessimistic about the expected outcomes of the reorganization process than they were in 1992. In the 1992 survey, only about 15% of the managers expected a clear deterioration due to the reorganization. In 1994, the percentage of managers in this category rose to 30%. In 1992, 27% of the managers were optimistic, expecting reorganization to have a positive effect on the farms. In 1994, the proportion of optimists dropped to 10%. The proportion of respondents who did not expect any changes as a result of reorganization or were undecided about its effects remained at around 60% in both surveys.

Table 3.4. Expected Changes as a Result of Farm-Enterprise Reorganization (percent of managers responding)

	Decrease		No change			
	1992	*1994*	*1992*	*1994*		
Total work force next year	30.0	33.3	48.8	56.4		
Administrative staff	59.7	64.6	34.6	31.2		
Production workers	43.6	53.0	39.9	40.9		
	Improve		Deteriorate		No change	
	1992	*1994*	*1992*	*1994*	*1992*	*1994*
Access to farm inputs	9.8	5.6	58.4	81.9	22.0	11.6
Access to credit	6.2	3.3	51.0	82.3	26.3	13.5
Marketing conditions	17.6	7.0	34.7	78.1	38	13.5
Conditions for household farming	41.2	33.0	13.5	14.4	40.8	52.5
Output	28.2	10.2	31.8	61.9	29.4	21.8
Degree of economic autonomy	54.3	63.3	5.3	6.5	27.8	19.1
Labor discipline	36.3	23.7	13.5	36.7	34.3	39.5

A significantly higher proportion of managers in 1994 expected deterioration in access to inputs, access to credit, marketing conditions, production, and labor discipline (Table 3.4). The proportion of managers who expected improvement in these areas as a result of reorganization was lower in 1994 than in 1992. Although managers reported that they experienced more economic autonomy (i.e., less interference from governmental officials) in their managerial decisions, the general pessimism suggests that autonomy is associated with loss of centralized support, rather than increased opportunity for initiative.

Production in Farm Enterprises

The value of output on the sample farms (averaged over the period 1990-1993) was approximately evenly split between livestock and crop products. The average gross product per farm (measured in constant 1983 prices) declined by more than 20% between 1990 and 1993 (Table 3.5). The decline was greatest in livestock production, as crop production decreased by around 10%. As a result, the product mix changed systematically over time, with the proportions of crops and livestock converging to 50% from opposite directions: the average proportion of crops in gross product rose from 44% in 1990 to 49% in 1993, while the proportion of livestock products declined accordingly from 56% in 1990 to 51% in 1993 (Table 3.6).

When output is measured in current prices, the proportion of crops increased from 35% of total sales in 1990 to 50% in 1993, with the proportion of livestock sales correspondingly declining from 65% to 50% (Table 3.6). Terms of trade shifted in favor of crop products over time, as the prices of crop products increased more rapidly than the prices of livestock products. The changes in the volume of production and in the structure of production and sales as reported by farm managers in the sample reflect general trends in the livestock sector in

Russia and other countries of the former Soviet Union since 1990.

Table 3.5. Production and Product Mix in Russian Farm Enterprises 1990-1994 (averages per farm for farms with data for all years, constant 1983 prices)

Year	Farms	Gross product	Crops	Livestock
1990	181	3617	1832	1790
1991	181	3362	1751	1618
1992	181	3067	1640	1428
1993	181	2875	1624	1256
1994	181	3160	1801	1361

Table 3.6. Structure of Production and Sales (in percent, average for the sample)

Year	Gross product in constant prices		Sales in current prices	
	Crops	Livestock	Crops	Livestock
1990	44	56	35	65
1991	47	53	35	65
1992	48	52	55	45
1993	49	51	50	50
1994	51	49	50	50
Average	**48**	**52**	**45**	**55**

Crops

Despite the reported loss of land to the state reserve and individual users, the total reported planted area in farm enterprises changed little between 1992 and 1993 (Table 3.7). This may be because traditional enterprises lease back some of the land that they formally allocate to the land reserve. Area planted to grain has declined on the sample farms from 76% of total cultivated area in 1992 to 68% in 1993, and area devoted to annual and perennial grasses has increased from 15% to 22% (Table 3.7). There has been no notable change in the other components of land use, such as sugar beets, sunflower, potatoes and vegetables, and orchards. Most of the area sown to grain on these sample farms remains under wheat (35% of total planted area).

Virtually all farm enterprises in the sample produce grain (mainly wheat and barley), as well as annual and perennial grasses for animal feed. Over 90% of farms meet their entire demand for hay from on-farm production, and over 80% of farms produce all of their needs in concentrated feed. Managers reported that prices of purchased feed were too high (80% of respondents), although at the time of the survey, managers could still sell a ton of grain and receive more than the purchase price of a ton of concentrate feed. By the end of 1994, the relative prices had shifted, and a ton of purchased concentrate feed cost more than a ton of average grain sold. Thus the tendency toward self-sufficiency in feed supply reported in the survey probably continued throughout 1994. Fewer

than half of the enterprises in the sample produced technical crops (sunflower and sugar beets), potatoes, and vegetables, and only 10 of 232 farms produced fruits commercially.

Most farm managers (65%-85%) reported that the main crops, including grain, sunflower, sugar beet, and fodder grasses, were profitable. On the other hand, potatoes and vegetables were viewed as unprofitable by 80% of respondents. Managers do not appear to make future production plans based on profitability, since the majority intended to make little change in the structure of production. Over 60% of the managers did not intend to adjust even the production of the relatively unprofitable crops (potatoes and vegetables). Only corn and sunflower were candidates for increased production in the future, probably because they were initially produced by a relatively small proportion of farms.

Table 3.7. Crop Production and Structure of Planted Area in Farm Enterprises: 1992-1993

	1992				1993			
	Producers, percent	*Harvest, ton*	*Planted area, ha*	*Planted area, %*	*Producers, percent*	*Harvest, ton*	*Planted area, ha*	*Planted area, %*
Wheat	90	2399	1358	35	98	3722	1407	34
All grains	90	6209	2945	76	98	7961	2824	68
Sunflower	44	849	266	7	47	736	294	7
Sugar beets	41	2034	67	2	34	5976	62	2
Potatoes	43	396	18	0.5	35	707	10	0.2
Vegetables	35	344	12	0.3	33	522	9	0.2
Fruits	3	1301	18	0.5	4	1211	12	0.3
Fodder beets	28	681	9	0.2	21	1077	6	0.1
Hay	90	1200	564	14	91	7467	915	22

Livestock

Virtually all farms in the sample produce milk and beef, and nearly two-thirds produce pork (Tables 3.8 and 3.9). The average per-farm production of the main livestock products (beef, milk, pork) declined between 1992 and 1993. The per-farm production of eggs and poultry, on the other hand, increased quite significantly, but the number of producers in the sample was small

compared to the number of producers of beef, milk, and pork.

Profitability of livestock products in late 1993 on the whole was judged to be slightly better than in 1992. Thus, 36% of managers viewed beef and milk, the main livestock products in the sample, as profitable in 1993, while in 1992 beef was viewed as profitable by 16% and milk by 27% of respondents. Nonetheless, 60%-90% of farm managers (depending on the particular product) reported that livestock production was unprofitable in 1993, and yet the majority expressed an intention to maintain livestock production at essentially the same level as in the past. Although managers in both surveys expressed an intention to keep livestock production roughly unchanged, the production of the main livestock products declined (Table 3.8), suggesting a lack of strategic vision with regard to adjustment in the livestock enterprise on these farms.

Table 3.8. Livestock Production in Farm Enterprises

Product	Percent of producers among sample farms		Average per producer, ton	
	1992	1993	1992	1993
Beef	97%	97%	206	141
Pork	65%	67%	82	58
Mutton	28%	27%	31	41
Eggs (pieces)	10%	14%	4081	7692
Poultry	10%	12%	159	272
Milk	96%	96%	1494	1400
Wool (kg)	NA	65%	NA	1700

Table 3.9. Number of Animals per Farm and per Producer

	Percent of farms with animals in each category	Average per farm in each category, head
Bulls over 1 yr	89%	208
Cows	96%	551
Heifers under 2 yrs	94%	254
Calves under 1 yr	94%	522
Pigs	70%	712
Piglets	61%	575
Sheep	28%	2400
Poultry	13%	70364

Labor

The average number of permanent workers per farm declined by 12% from 344 in 1990 to 302 in 1993 (Table 3.10). This was the result of an across-the-board decrease in the number of

employed in all occupations. In each survey, about 11% of permanent employees worked in administration, and about the same proportion worked in non-agricultural production, such as construction, maintenance, and processing. The number of workers in the social sphere and the number of seasonal workers (neither of these categories is included in the count of permanent workers) fell particularly sharply (by nearly 30%).

Table 3.10. Labor Resources in Russian Farm Enterprises: 1990-1993 (per farm averages)

	1990	1993
Total permanent workers	344	302
Of which:		
Agricultural production	77%	78%
Non-agricultural production	12%	11%
Administration	11%	11%
Workers in the social sphere	22	16
Pensioners	35	34
Seasonal workers	21	15

Table 3.11. Wages in Russian Farm Enterprises, October 1993 (thou. rubles)

	Monthly wages
Average wage	**43.7**
Combine operators	81.0
Managers	75.1
Chief specialists	58.2
Drivers	57.1
Specialists	41.4
Milking personnel	38.9
Other livestock workers	34.6
Administrative staff	27.2
Unskilled labor	22.0

The structure of employment changed little with the reduction in numbers employed. Half of those employed in agriculture continued to produce crops, and the other half continued with livestock. Among those employed in non-agricultural production, the number of workers in processing on the farm remained unchanged, while the work force in other non-agricultural activities declined. This produced an increase in the proportion of workers employed in processing of agricultural products (from 15% of all employed in non-agricultural production in 1990 to 20% in 1993).

The average monthly salary of farm workers in October 1993 was 44 thou. rubles according to the managers' responses. There was considerable variability among different occupations; combine operators and managers earned nearly double the average salary, while administrative staff and unskilled workers earned half the average salary (Table 3.11). Over 70% of farm managers reported that the available labor was sufficient for their needs. Seasonal shortages are typically resolved by hiring temporary help (in over 60% of the farms). Only 4% of respondents reported excessive or redundant labor on their farms. Ten percent of managers reported that they would fire excess workers if they had any.

Farm enterprises have difficulties meeting the payroll. Over 80% of managers reported that salary payment was delayed in some months of 1993 (compared to 53% of managers in the 1992 survey). The main reason for salary delays was shortage of funds to meet the payroll bill (92% of respondents who were forced to delay salaries). The preferred strategy for dealing with shortage of funds for payroll was to delay salary payment until funds became available (90% of respondents) or to borrow (50%). Only 10%-15% of respondents reported that they would lay workers off, cut salaries, or transfer employees to work outside the farm enterprise if problems arose meeting payrolls. Managers in both the 1992 and 1994 surveys thus reported a continued and consistent reluctance to shed labor under any circumstances (Table 3.12).

The proportion of wages and salaries in total farm expenditure increased to 38% in 1993, continuing a trend observed in the 1992 survey, in which the share of salaries increased from 28% in 1990 to 34% in 1992 (Fig. 3.4). This finding derives from a subset of 122 farm enterprises that participated in both surveys, and thus it is more robust than comparison of the expenditure proportions in the sample as a whole. Thus, even though aggregate data show farm wages declining dramatically in real terms and relative to wages in other sectors (see Fig. 1.4), wages continue to grow as a share of farm expenditures on large enterprises.

Table 3.12. Management Strategies: What to Do If No Money to Meet Payroll? (percent of managers responding)

	Yes		No	
	1992	1994	1992	1994
Dismiss some workers	13.2	16.2	80.6	83.8
Keep workers, reduce wages	7.8	12.4	87.2	87.6
Delay wage payments	57.0	90.6	39.1	9.4
Delay other payments	64.7	--	31.4	--
Take debt	69.8	50.4	27.9	49.6
Shift workers to outside jobs	8.9	11.5	82.2	88.5

Fig. 3.4. Proportion of Farm Wages in Total Expenditure*

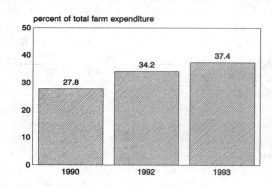

percent of total farm expenditure

* Based on matched sample of 122 farms from two surveys.

Farm Inputs and Services

Managers reported that farms continue to purchase most of their inputs through state channels (Table 3.13). The firms characterized as state channels are probably the privatized successors of the former state supply agencies, but are perceived by managers to be still part of state channels. Alternative supply channels are emerging in the form of commercial private entrepreneurs, farmers' cooperatives, and other farm enterprises acting as suppliers. Private entrepreneurs are active in the supply of spare parts, construction materials and services, and young animals. Other farm enterprises supply the inputs listed above, and also seeds and seedlings, animal feed, and farm machinery. The "other sources" column in Table 3.13 probably represents cases in which the farm enterprise produces or generates its own inputs services. Farm enterprises have traditionally relied on themselves for seeds and seedlings, feed, young animals, construction, and especially mechanical field services. In response to a specific question, 88% of farm managers reported that mechanical field services are carried out using the farm's own machinery and equipment. Leasing of equipment became somewhat more widespread in 1994, but at

the time of this sample and in the farms surveyed leasing was rare.

The phenomenon of farm enterprises acting as suppliers of inputs and services was recorded in the earlier survey, and this marks a change from the economic behavior of farms prior to the reforms. Under the centralized administrative system, farms had little incentive to sell services or inputs to each other, since the cost of carrying inventories of inputs was low. Although farm enterprises always supplied inputs and services to employees for use on household plots, commercial supply to other enterprises and to private farms is a development new to the period of market reforms. Table 3.14 lists the responses of farm managers who sell inputs and farm services to other enterprises, and also to private farmers and household plots. In addition to commercial relations between farm enterprises, voluntary cooperation between farm enterprises in the purchase and use of inputs appears to be increasing (Table 3.15).

Table 3.13. Access to Different Supply Channels for Farm Inputs and Services
(percent of 234 respondents who report using the channels)

Input/Service	State channels	Consumer coops	Private sources	Farmers' coops	Other enterprises	Other sources
Seeds, seedlings	67.1	4.7	2.6	0.9	25.6	15.0
Feed	30.8	0.4	2.6	1.3	10.3	12.4
Young animals	32.1	3.0	11.5	0.4	16.7	11.5
Mineral fertilizer	80.8	5.1	0.4	0.4	5.1	0.9
Herbicides/Pesticides	81.2	3.0	0.9	0.4	6.0	1.3
Machinery/equipment	92.3	10.7	6.0	3.0	14.5	6.0
Repairs/maintenance	54.3	--	4.3	0.9	9.8	7.7
Spare parts	96.6	17.5	39.7	5.6	33.8	6.8
Fuel	98.7	2.1	9.4	1.7	8.1	9.4
Mechanical field works	28.2	0.9	3.4	1.7	9.8	11.1
Veterinary medicines	95.7	3.0	1.7	0.4	6.0	4.7
Veterinary services	59.8	--	2.1	--	5.1	9.4
Construction materials	87.6	--	23.5	3.0	32.1	12.8
Construction services	29.1	1.7	22.2	0.4	6.0	11.1
Consulting	63.7	2.6	10.3	1.3	16.7	5.1

Table 3.14. Enterprises Acting as Suppliers of Farm Inputs (percent of 234 farm enterprises)

Input/Service	To other enterprises	To private farmers	To household plots
Seeds, seedlings	36.8	47.9	44.9
Feed	25.6	13.7	82.1
Young animals	31.2	26.9	82.1
Organic fertilizer	6.4	6.8	38.0
Mineral fertilizer	1.3	2.6	6.4
Herbicides/pesticides	2.6	4.3	28.6
Machinery/equipment	17.9	35.9	41.9
Repairs/maintenance	9.8	25.6	31.2
Spare parts	16.2	18.4	17.9
Fuel	8.1	9.4	29.5
Mechanical field services	19.7	47.0	84.6
Veterinary medicines	4.3	26.5	62.4
Veterinary services	6.0	40.2	85.0
Construction materials	15.4	15.4	81.6
Construction services	5.6	5.6	54.3
Consulting	27.4	45.7	69.7

Managers reported that inputs are too expensive, and the frequency of complaints about input prices was substantially higher than in 1992 (Table 3.16). As a result, the proportion of respondents reporting that they experience no problems with the purchase of inputs declined relative to the previous survey. Physical shortages of inputs were not reported to be a problem in 1992, and were reported to be even less so in 1994. Affordability and profitability, rather than availability, constrains use of inputs on the large enterprises.

Virtually all farm managers (98%) reported that they provide services to their employees in working their household plots, and over 70% provide services to private farmers in the area. The range of farm services provided to employees, other village residents (such as teachers, doctors, postal workers, etc.), and even private farmers is broad in scope (Table 3.17). In addition to leasing farm machinery for work in the small fields of individual producers who do not have mechanical equipment of their own, farm enterprises also sell used farm equipment to their employees, private farmers, and

other individual operators (respectively 50%, 40%, and 33% of farm enterprises in the sample). Farm managers reported that they did not provide credit to employees or other rural residents.

Table 3.15. Cooperation in Purchase and Use of Inputs (percent of 234 respondents)

Input/Service	Percent
Seeds, seedlings	12.8
Organic fertilizers	1.7
Mineral fertilizers	9.8
Herbicides/Pesticides	11.1
Machinery/equipment	6.8
Spare parts	12.4
Veterinary medicine	8.1
Construction materials	10.3
Fuel	8.1

Two-thirds of the respondents indicated that their employees have priority in access to farm services and are charged preferential rates for these services. Pensioners, on the other hand, enjoy preferential terms on only half of farms.

Table 3.16. Reported Difficulties in Purchase of Farm Inputs (percent of respondents for each input/service)

Input	Price too high		Not available		No problems	
	1992	1994	1992	1994	1992	1994
Seed	23.1	45.7	2.3	3.0	28.1	18.4
Fertilizer	68.1	91.0	1.9	0.9	19.2	5.6
Herbicides/pesticides	60.8	89.3	5.8	1.3	21.2	5.1
Machinery/equipment	--	94.9	--	--	--	4.3
Spare parts	52.7	85.5	19.6	1.3	21.9	11.5
Veterinary medicines	39.6	71.8	13.8	3.0	36.9	19.7
Construction materials	61.2	87.6	12.7	1.7	19.6	8.5
Fuel	--	78.6	--	0.4	--	17.9
Mean of responses	**50.9**	**80.6**	**9.4**	**1.7**	**24.5**	**11.3**

Table 3.17. Services Supplied by Farm Enterprises to Rural Residents
(percent of 234 farm enterprises supplying the services to each recipient category)

Services	Employees	Other Villagers	Private Farmers
Farm machinery for contract work	98.7	85.9	49.1
Transport	99.1	85.9	41.9
Pasture and hay	90.2	72.2	26.9
Consulting	76.5	66.2	51.3
Credit	18.4	2.6	0.4
Veterinary services	92.7	80.3	53.0
Product marketing	66.7	45.3	12.4
Fuel for farm uses	33.8	15.8	12.4
Construction materials	85.9	49.1	17.5
Heating fuel	46.6	26.5	7.3

Marketing

The large farm enterprises have a clear commercial orientation: virtually all producers in each product category reported commercial sales of more than 80% of output of most products (Table 3.18). A notable exception is grain, where half the output is used internally, largely as feed for livestock. Potatoes, fruits, and vegetables are also consumed on farm in relatively large proportions.

The marketing situation remains basically as in the previous survey. State procurement agencies or their privatized successors retain a dominant role as the main marketing channel for most products (Table 3.19). Notable exceptions are potatoes, vegetables, fruits, and eggs: these products are often sold directly to consumers in farmers' markets or to other enterprises. Despite the dominance of state marketing channels, farm managers believe that they have access to alternative channels for sale of their products, should such a need arise (Table 3.19).

Managers reported that the main marketing difficulties for farm products were low prices and late payment by large monopolistic buyers (Table 3.20). Few managers complained of difficulty finding buyers for their produce, or of difficulties with transport and delivery.

The respondents were on the whole highly pessimistic in their evaluation of the marketing situation. Only 5% of farm managers rated the situation as average or good. Fully 95% of the respondents characterized the marketing situation as poor, primarily due to low prices of farm products. These results are similar to the 1992 survey, when the respondents also complained of low prices. However, the overall evaluation became more pessimistic between 1992 and 1994: the marketing situation was rated average or good by 13% of respondents in 1992, compared to only 5% in 1994. A very small number of managers (14) indicated that they export some of their output directly. Half of these reported that they had great difficulty securing export licenses. The precise nature (whether national or provincial) of the export licenses is not clear from the replies.

Table 3.18. Proportion of Output Consumed and Sold by Producers (in percent)

	Number of producers*		Proportion of output sold	
	total	reporting sales	all producers	producers reporting sales
Crops:				
Grain	231	225	49	50
Sunflower	109	92	69	83
Potatoes	75	41	35	63
Sugar beet	74	52	59	85
Vegetables	73	37	38	74
Fruit&berries	10	7	44	63
Livestock:				
Meat	231	229	82	83
Milk	224	222	81	81
Wool	64	61	95	100
Eggs	32	25	63	80

* Out of total of 234 sample farms.

Table 3.19. Main Marketing Channel by Commodity (percent of total number of responses for each commodity)

Commodity	Number of farms reporting sales	Procurement firms*	Collective farms and other enterprises	Direct sales	Availability of alternative channels#
Grain	225	91.1	6.6	0.9	48
Sunflower	92	72.8	21.8	3.3	67.4
Sugar beet	52	86.5	5.8	5.7	17.3
Meat	229	95.6	0.4	1.3	57.2
Milk	222	94.1	0.9	2.7	29.3
Potatoes	41	46.4	21.9	24.4	46.3
Vegetables	37	35.1	8.1	45.9	64.9
Fruits	7	28.6	28.6	42.9	57.1
Eggs	25	56	24	12	56
Wool	61	85.2	3.3	3.3	26.2

* The traditional procurement firms have been privatized, and buy as agents of state procurement, as well as on their own account.
# Percent of commercial producers in each category answering 'yes' to the question "Can you choose a buyer for the given product?"

Table 3.20. Marketing Problems as Reported by Farm-Enterprise Managers
(percent of total number of responses in each commodity category)

Commodity	Number of responses	Reported Problems				
		Late payment	Low price	No buyer	Delivery difficulties	Other
Grain	225	92.9	92.4	48.9	10.7	3.6
Sunflower	92	78.3	93.5	34.8	9.8	3.3
Sugar beet	52	59.6	82.7	36.5	40.4	5.8
Meat	229	83.4	95.6	44.1	7.9	2.2
Milk	222	84.7	97.3	50.9	9.0	2.3
Potatoes	41	43.9	65.9	43.9	7.3	--
Vegetables	37	54.1	73.0	48.6	13.5	5.4
Fruits & Berries	7	42.9	42.9	71.4	--	--
Eggs	25	60.0	60.0	40.0	4.0	--
Wool	61	77.0	91.8	59.0	8.2	6.6

Processing

Few farms are reported to have significant processing capacity, although farm managers in contexts outside the survey frequently express a desire to process their own products, and avoid what are perceived to be high marketing and processing margins. Around 10% of managers reported that they had a bakery, a small flour mill, a vegetable oil press, or a dairy processing plant (Table 3.21). Only 5% of managers reported capacity to process meat. Over 20% of managers reported that they had a facility for manufacturing their own concentrated feed.

Although farms in the sample do not process much of their own products, they distribute processed products received from processors in lieu of monetary payments for delivery of raw materials (Table 3.22). Payment in kind is mainly received in the form of concentrated feed, sugar, meat, and dairy products (around 20%-30% of farms have such arrangements). The annual quantities of these products are not large except for concentrate feed, and they are used primarily for on-farm consumption, not for resale.

Table 3.21. Processing Facilities in Farm Enterprises

Facility	Percent of farms	Average capacity, ton/year
Bakery	12.8	836
Concentrated feed mill	21.8	3456
Flour mill	7.7	933
Vegetable oil	10.7	310
Canning	1.3	1662
Meat processing	5.1	120
Dairy products	8.5	394

Table 3.22. Payment in Kind to Farms from Processors

Product	Percent of farms	Average quantity, ton/year
Flour	17.9	69
Concentrated feed	22.2	1262
Starch	10.7	88
Sugar	26.9	103
Vegetable oil	16.7	31
Meat products	18.4	10
Dairy products	27.8	23

Social Services and Benefits

The proportion of managers reporting that their farm enterprises provide various social services and benefits to employees dropped for most categories of services and benefits between 1992 and 1994. The change in the overall frequency of provision of services and benefits is observed both in the full sample and in the matched subsample of 122 farm managers who participated in the two surveys (their responses are shown in Fig. 3.5). Provision of housing by farm enterprises and rent subsidies declined because of the overall tendency to privatize apartments and houses to residents. Other benefits related to housing, such as supply of heating fuel at preferential prices and subsidized utilities, also declined. Farms have also reduced their contributions to education, as can be seen in cutbacks of day care and school subsidies. The primary financial responsibility for education even prior to the reforms was with the government, not the farms, although farms provided financial support and support in kind, such as maintenance of school buildings, provision of heat, and supply of food for cafeterias where these operated. Augmentation of employee pensions has all but disappeared. Although the number of services provided has declined, 60% of the farms and more still provide benefits shown in Fig. 3.5 (down from 75% to 95% in 1992). This decline in provision of social services and benefits is probably a reflection of the deteriorating economic situation of the farm enterprises. As wages grow in proportion to total expenditures and wage arrears accumulate, expenditures for social services are squeezed.

Despite the obvious difficulties in financing social services, farm managers did not report much transfer of responsibility for social assets to local authorities. Only 40% of respondents in 1994 reported that some social assets had been transferred to the village council. This is similar to the situation observed in the 1992 survey. There has been only a slight increase between 1992 and 1994 in the proportion of farms that transferred social

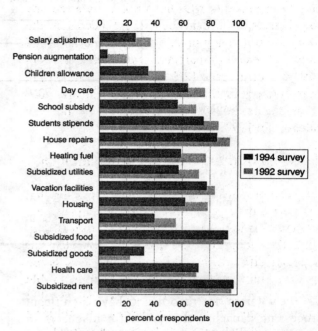

Fig. 3.5. Provision of Social Services and Benefits: 1992-1994

assets in each specific category (Table 3.23). Day care centers, schools, clinics, and clubs appear to be the first candidates for transfer to the local council. The responsibility for roads and utility systems is retained by the farm enterprise in virtually all cases.

Table 3.23. Transfer of Social Assets to Local Council*

	Transferred	
	1992	1994
Housing	8.5	5.1
Day care centers	18.4	29.5
Schools	17.4	26.9
Clinics	--	19.2
Shops	--	7.7
Clubs	18.8	28.6
Sports facilities	--	4.3
Sewage/water	4.3	3.4
Electric/power	6.2	7.7
Telephones	6.2	9.4
Roads	4.6	5.1

* Percent of 260 managers in 1992 and 234 managers in 1994.

Sixty percent of all respondents and over 70% of the respondents who have not transferred any social assets to the local council responded that "the local authorities are unable to maintain the social assets." The cost of maintaining the social assets in 1993 was on average 12% of overall expenditure in farm enterprises, the same as in 1992. Nearly 50% of managers did not expect a change in this cost category in 1994.

Perceived Difficulties During Reorganization

The proportion of respondents reporting that the process of reorganization is proceeding with "no problems" is less than 50%: it ranges from 20% to 50% depending on the particular problem of potential difficulties addressed. These results are virtual identical to those of the 1992 survey (Table 3.24). Yet more managers in 1994 than in 1992 diagnosed certain areas as "severe difficulties": thus, 40% of managers viewed debt repayment as a severe problem (compared to less than 20% in 1992); nearly 50% of managers viewed subsidies to the social sphere as a severe problem (compared to less than 30% in 1992). The proportion of managers that diagnosed other areas as problematic (although not necessarily severe) is on the whole somewhat higher in 1994 than in 1992. The proportion of managers identifying problems with information and understanding the laws and decrees pertaining to reorganization did not increase and even slightly decreased between the two surveys (Table 3.24).

Finance and Credit

Virtually all farms in the sample have some outstanding debt. The average per-farm debt in the first quarter of 1994 was under 250 million rubles, compared to average assets of 1-1.5 billion rubles. Nearly 80% of farms borrowed short-term in 1993 (100 million rubles per farm), but only 10% of farms managed to obtain medium- or long-term loans (also 100 million rubles per borrowing farm). About half the managers reported that during reorganization debt will be divided between the recipients of farm shares or between the new autonomous subdivisions within the farm. In about 40% of responses, however, the managers ignored the impact of outstanding debt on reorganization and did not propose any solution to this problem (Table 3.25).

Table 3.24. Perceived Difficulties During Reorganization (percent of 234 respondents)

	Severe difficulties		Some difficulties		No problem	
	1992	1994	1992	1994	1992	1994
Access to information about new laws/decrees	25.0	30.8	41.9	30.3	26.5	28.0
Understanding of new laws by employees	50.4	43.2	29.2	33.3	13.8	22.2
Division of land into shares	24.2	22.2	31.5	38.5	35.0	37.6
Determination of asset shares	23.8	21.4	40.8	44.0	25.4	32.9
Distribution of assets to shareholders	--	28.2	--	34.2	--	35.9
Repayment of debt	18.1	38.5	25.8	20.1	45.4	39.7
Subsidies to social sphere	28.8	47.4	26.2	26.9	36.9	24.4
Allocation of shares to pensioners	12.7	13.7	25.8	30.8	52.3	53.8
Allocation of shares to former employees	17.7	22.2	19.6	22.2	53.1	48.7
Privatization of housing	27.7	22.2	23.5	28.2	41.2	48.7
Allocation of shares to employees of social sphere	16.2	23.9	23.5	24.4	50.8	50.0

Table 3.25. "What to Do with Farm Debt During Reorganization?" (percent of responses counting multiple answers)

	1994	1992
Leave everything as previously	40	41
Write off debt	7	2
Divide between shareholders	39	26
Divide between new subdivisions	8	12
Other	6	19

Table 3.26. Loan Collateral Used by Farm Managers: 1992-1994 (percent of respondents who borrow)

Form of Collateral	1994	1992
Land	34	24
Machines	61	44
Crops	26	83
Government guarantees	28	NA
Buildings	4	41
Cosigners	3	9
No collateral	15	NA

Credit is mostly secured by guarantees: only 15% of farm managers who borrowed reported that no guarantee was required. The prevalent form of guarantee is a lien on machinery and equipment (over 60% of borrowers). Crops are used as collateral by one quarter of farm managers, and nearly 30% of managers cited government obligations as collateral. In 1992, managers reported that crops and buildings were accepted as collateral, while in 1994 machinery and equipment were pledged more frequently (Table 3.26). The banking system may thus be shifting toward forms of collateral that are at the same time more secure and more liquid: machines are more secure than crops and more easily liquidated than buildings.

Contrary to indications from the banking system that banks do not yet accept land as collateral, one third of farm managers reported that they use land to secure loans. This is consistent with the 1992 survey, where a quarter of the managers indicated that land was used as collateral (Table 3.26). Farm managers' reports that they use

land as collateral differ sharply from those of private farmers, only 2% of whom indicated that they use land as collateral.

The reported interest rate was practically the same for short-term and long-term borrowing (155% and 171% per annum, respectively; the difference between the interest rates is not statistically significant). Most managers reported borrowing at 212%-213% per annum (half short-term borrowers and 60% of long-term borrowers reported this interest rate). Approximately 20% of borrowers managed to get short-term loans at 28% per annum, which was probably a special credit program of the government.

Although these nominal interest rates were deeply negative in real terms under the conditions of Russian inflation, they were perceived by the borrowers to be prohibitively high. Three-quarters of farm managers reported that they could not afford to borrow what they needed for normal farm operation because the interest rates were too high. Fewer than 20% of managers identified credit shortages as an obstacle to adequate borrowing. Overall, some 80% of managers complained of difficulties obtaining credit (both short-term and long-term).

In the managers' view, the traditional farm enterprises, such as collective enterprises, kolkhozes, and sovkhozes, were likely to have the greatest difficulties with access to credit in 1994 (45% of respondents). New enterprises, such as joint stock companies or new cooperatives were perceived as having potentially less difficulty with credit (25%-30% of respondents), while associations of private farmers and small agribusiness entrepreneurs were considered able to borrow with very little difficulty (19% and 8% of respondents, respectively). Less than 30% of respondents believed that all agents would have equal access to credit in 1994 (Table 3.27). Eighty percent of farm managers reported a perception that private farmers would have equal or better access to credit than collective enterprises (Table 3.28).

Table 3.27. "What Farm Structures will Have the Greatest Difficulty Obtaining Credit Next Year?" (percent of respondents in each category)

	1994	1992
Kolkhozes/sovkhozes	46	35
Collective enterprises	46	24
Farmers' cooperatives	24	15
Closed joint-stock companies	26	16
Open joint-stock companies	30	12
Associations of private farms	19	9
Small agribusiness entrepreneurs	8	NA
Equal access for all	29	25

Table 3.28. Anticipated Access to Credit for Private Farmers Compared to Collectives (percent of respondents)

	1994	1992
Easier than for collectives	42	67
About the same as for collectives	40	13
More difficult that for collectives	4	7
Undecided	14	13

Managers in the 1992 survey also perceived that private farmers would have preferential access to credit. The survey data confirm the managers' perception at least with regard to interest rates. Nearly 70% of private farmers in the survey reported that they borrowed in 1993 at annual interest rates below 30%, while half of farm managers reported paying interest rates of slightly above 200% annually. The survey data do not offer insight into the degree of rationing of credit at various interest rates and among various borrowers.

The outstanding debt of farm enterprises was offset to a certain extent by their receivables, which averaged 140 million per farm. Since the average outstanding debt was 250 million per farm, this reduced the net indebtedness to slightly over 100 million rubles in the first quarter of 1994. The main debtors were the state procurement organizations, which accounted for nearly 60% of accounts receivable, and the processors, which accounted for

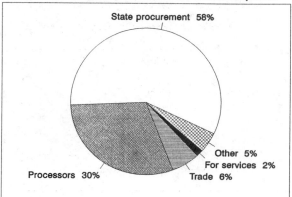

Fig. 3.6. Accounts Receivable of Farm Enterprises

30% of the amounts owed to farm enterprises (Fig. 3.6). The level of receivables at 140 million rubles per farm should be compared to the level of 1993 sales at current prices, which averaged 350 million rubles per farm, or 2.5 times the receivables. Arrears thus represent approximately 150 days of sales. Calculation of the time in arrears for each farm in the sample indicates that receivables amounted on average to four months of sales across all farms (126 days).

Both calculations suggest that delayed payment was definitely a problem in an inflationary environment. Farms were able to finance accounts receivable, but did not receive interest although they had to pay interest on their loans. The state was the main debtor (through the procurement organizations), and obligations undertaken by the farms were used in part to finance accounts receivable. Political pressures to relieve farm debts by rescheduling centralized credits at the end of 1994 were thus heightened by the government's perceived dual position in the farm finance problem, as both debtor and creditor. If the procurement firms are in fact privatized, then the government is not responsible for their obligations, but farm managers in 1994 perceived the procurement firms to be owned by the state or acting on the state's behalf.

4. Farm Employees

At the time of the survey in early 1994, most employees of farm enterprises were the same people who had worked on the predecessor collective or state farms. Farm employees appeared better informed about the process of reorganization than in 1992, but had little optimism that their personal economic welfare would improve in the future. Despite the general pessimism about the future prospects for the farm enterprise, fewer employees than in 1992 indicated intentions to become private farmers at any point in the future. Farm employees continued to work in much the traditional patterns of the Soviet era, relying on a combination of wages from the enterprise and earnings in money and kind from household production. Households specialized in livestock production, as in the past, and marketed much of their surplus directly to consumers on local markets.

The farm employees in the sample thus do not show much change in their economic behavior from that of the pre-reform period. Yet these employees are not elderly widows or marginally employable unskilled workers. According to the demographic profile of the sample, many employees on farm enterprises in the sample are men and women in their thirties and forties with high school education or more schooling. Interviews with these employees lead to the conclusion that the reforms introduced at the farm level up to the time of this survey (early 1994) had not created opportunities either within the traditional enterprises or outside them to mobilize the efforts and talents of this important group of rural people.

Demographic Profile

The average family of an employee in the sample consists of 3.7 persons, with 80% of the families concentrated in the range of between 3 and 5 persons. Most of the families include a husband and wife with children. Only 10 out of 507 respondents are single (evenly divided between males and females). In 85% of cases the head of the household is identified as male, and in the remainder the head is female. The head of household is on average 40 years old, and the spouse is 37. Nearly 40% of family members in the sample are children and young people under age 20 (Fig. 4.1). The number of older people over 60 in the sample is only 4%. Since the sample included only active employees and their household members, most retired people were excluded. The demographic profile of employees is thus not that of the village as a whole, although it is likely to represent that of the agricultural work force.

Table 4.1. Ownership of Housing in Employee Families (percent of households)

	Owned by		
	family	farm enterprise	village council
Separate house	78	20	0
Apartment			
in small building	60	36	1
in large block	24	60	7

Nearly 60% of the families live in separate houses. Thirty percent live in an apartment in a small building (2-4 apartments), and only 10% reported that they live in an apartment in a large building. Families own their homes in 65% of the cases, and live in housing owned by the farm enterprise in 30% of the cases. Most separate

Fig. 4.1. Age Distribution in Employee Households

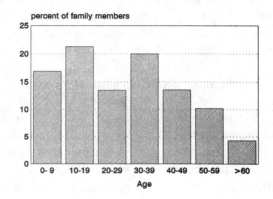

houses (80%) are privately owned, and 35% of apartments in small buildings are owned by the farm enterprises, as are 60% of apartments in large blocks (Table 4.1). Most housing is more than 10 years old (70% of the respondents), and only 10% of families live in housing built 1-5 years ago.

A typical farm-enterprise employee has lived in a rural area since birth (80% of respondents). Mobility in rural areas is low: 75% of respondents have lived in the same village for more than 10 years. Both the head of household and the spouse have basically the same education (Table 4.2). Most of the employees are high-school graduates (general or technical schools) and about 15% report some higher education.

Although the level of educational attainment is approximately the same for both spouses, occupations differ (Table 4.3). While 90% of heads of household reported that they work full time on the farm enterprise, only 60% of spouses work full time on the enterprise, and fully one third of the spouses reported that they do not work at all on the farm. Among the spouses who do not work on the farm enterprise, one half work in the village (teachers, doctors, etc.), one fifth are pensioners and another fifth are housewives. The rest work in other enterprises or study. The head of the household is typically a skilled worker (55%) or a manager or specialist (20%) in the farm enterprise. The occupations of spouses are more diversified. While some of them are also skilled workers and managers or specialists (around 30% in both categories, less than half the frequency among heads of household), nearly 40% work in administration or the social sphere. Seven percent of the spouses report their occupation as "housewife." The percentage of pensioners among spouses is understandably higher, as women retire at an earlier age (55 compared to 60 for men).

Employees and Farm Reorganization

Virtually all the employees (95%) reported that their farm enterprises had reorganized. Nearly 40% of respondents characterized their reorganized farms as collective enterprises, cooperatives, or partnerships. Another 15% reported that their farms

were traditional collective farms (*kolkhoz*). In one third of the cases the farm was described as a closed joint-stock company. The responses of employees regarding farm organization are consistent with those of farm managers (see Table 3.1 in Chapter 3).

Table 4.2. Education Profile of Employee Families (percent of respondents)

	Head of Household	Spouse
Higher education	17	12
Secondary education	60	65
Uncompleted secondary (8 grades or less)	19	21
Professional courses	3	1
Illiterate	0	0
Number of persons	*507*	*497*

Table 4.3. Occupation Profile of Employee Families (percent of respondents)

	Head of household	Spouse
Works at farm enterprise		
Full time	90	61
Part time	2	3
Not at all	7	33
Manager/specialist	22	11
Skilled worker	54	18
Unskilled worker	8	6
Non-ag occupation	11	37
Administrative staff	4	10
Social sphere (farm)	2	10
Social sphere (village)	5	17
Other employment	2	5
Housewife	0	7
Pensioner	2	8
Number of persons	*507*	*497*

In the farms that decided to reorganize, 95% of the employees received land shares and 90% received asset shares. Farm managers similarly reported that land and asset shares had been allocated in 90% of the farms. The average land share reported by employees is around 20 ha, but more than a quarter of recipients reported that they did not know what their land share was (farm managers reported an average land share of 12.5 ha on a much wider base). Only 6% of respondents reported that they had received an actual plot of land in the process of reorganization. Most of these plots, however, are between 0.1 and 0.9 ha, so that even these few respondents may have been reporting additional allocation of land to their subsidiary household plots rather than receipt of land in the process of distribution of shares.

For half of respondents the value of asset shares was determined in 1992. The average value of an asset share calculated in 1992 was 54,000 rubles (approximately US$220 at the prevailing exchange rate of 250 rubles per US$ in the third quarter of 1992). The managers report an average value of 70,000 rubles (approximately US$280) for asset shares allocated in 1992. The same managers report that the average value of an asset share at the time of the survey (first quarter of 1994) was 2.2 million rubles, or $1500 at the prevailing exchange rate of about 1500 rubles per $US. Thus, the average ruble value of asset shares increased 30-fold since 1992 due to inflationary adjustments, and the dollar equivalent value increased 5-fold due to appreciation in the value of the ruble relative to the dollar. The whole notion of the value of asset shares appears to be fairly vague, and fully 53% of employees who had received asset shares did not know their value. The shares remain strictly in the form of paper certificates, as few people in the sample received assets in kind or redeemed the asset shares for cash.

Family Income

Farm employees derive income from wages and production on household plots, as well as pensions and other transfers. The earnings in agriculture did not catch up with inflation in 1993. The reported salaries in October 1993 were higher than the salaries in October 1992 by a factor of 8 (35,535 rubles compared to 4456 rubles), while consumer prices in Russia increased by a factor of 10 during the corresponding period. In November 1993, the average salary as reported by employees

was 36,000 rubles, compared to 44,000 rubles as reported by farm managers (in unmatched samples). The exchange rate at the time was approximately 1200 rubles per $US. Employees reported a very wide range in monthly salaries, from 2300 rubles to 300,000 rubles (the range of salaries reported by managers was between 7700 rubles and 162,000 rubles).

Table 4.4. Salary Delays in Farm Enterprises, 1992-1993

	1993	*1992*
Managers		
Salary delays occurred, %	80	53
Employees		
At least one instance of salary delay, %	60	44
Six or more instances of salary delay, %	8	4
Salary delays every month, %	5	0

Because of financial difficulties in the farm sector, salaries are not paid regularly. Over 60% of employees reported that salaries were delayed on at least one occasion in 1993, and 10% of employees reported that salaries were delayed on six or more occasions in 1993. Over 80% of farm managers indicated that there were some months with salary delays in 1993. These responses suggest increasing financial stress in farm enterprises. In the 1992 survey only 50% of managers and 40% of employees reported salary delays (Table 4.4). The full distribution of the number of months with salary delays reported by employees in 1993 is definitely worse than in 1992.

Salaries are traditionally augmented by payment in kind and by opportunities to purchase various commodities from the farm enterprise at preferential prices (Table 4.5). Almost everyone (over 90% of respondents) reported access to grain from the farm enterprise, either in payment in kind or at a nominal price. Grain is used for animal feed in household production, and is supplemented by access to hay (29% of respondents) and concentrate feed (13%). Employees also reported that they received or purchased sugar (44% of respondents), vegetable oil (30%), and meat (24%) from the farm.

Table 4.5. Supplementary Income in Kind Paid to Employees in 1993

	Total employees paid, percent	Payment in kind		Purchase from farm enterprise	
		percent of respondents	quantity, kg	percent of respondents	quantity, kg
Grain	91	30	1900	71	2900
Hay	29	13	2900	18	3500
Concentrated feed	13	4	840	9	422
Sugar	44	5	57	42	76
Vegetable oil	31	0	14	31	14
Meat	24	2	12	21	31

Household production is an important supplementary source of income for farm employees. Over 50% of families reported deriving more than one quarter of their income from household plots. Approximately 80% of families derive half or less of their income from subsidiary farming. The importance of household production as a source of supplementary income is consistent with previous findings.

Plot Structure and Tenure

Land formally designated as the household plot remains at less than half a hectare in most cases, and household production thus continues to be intensive and subsidiary to wage work on the farm enterprise. The average household plot in 1994 is 0.33 ha as reported by farm employees and 0.38 ha as reported by farm managers (using full unmatched samples). The change in plot sizes between the two surveys (1992 and 1994) is not statistically significant judging by the responses of either employees or managers. The change since 1990, however, is significant: the average plot size increased by more than 45%, from 0.24 ha in 1990 to 0.35 ha in 1992/1994. This average is based on the pooled responses of all managers and employees in the two surveys.

The increase in plot size varies across provinces (Table 4.6). Thus, the household plots in Novosibirsk and Saratov provinces hardly changed between 1990 and 1994 according to the managers, while the plot sizes in Orel and Rostov showed a substantial increase. The inferred increase is particularly large in Pskov Province, but here the observations are few in number and are all concentrated in a single district, producing curiously large average plots of over 1.5 ha (compared to 0.3-0.4 ha for the entire sample).

Table 4.6. Household Plots as Reported by Russian Managers and Employees (1992 and 1994 surveys, in hundredths of ha)

	Managers: pooled sample		Employees: different samples	
	1990	1992/94	1992	1994
All oblasts	23.7	39.3	29.9	33.2
W/out Pskov	22.9	32.5	26.9	24.1
Novosibirsk	14.2	15.3	20.9	16.2
Orel	36.5	59.2	40.7	37.0
Pskov	40.4	175.4	112.9	176.4
Rostov	26.2	43.1	37.2	32.2
Saratov	15.9	17.1	12.9	13.9

The average household plot is mostly arable land (65% of average plot size), with some hayland (20%), pasture (5%), and land used for growing fruits and berries (5%). Although household plots are intended to become private property, only 25% of the plots were fully privately owned at the time of the survey, while nearly 60% of the households did not report any privately owned land. In an average plot, 45% of land was privately owned, another 40% was held in usership, and 15% in lifetime inheritable possession (Table 4.7). The proportion of leased land in household plots was negligible. Compared to 1992, there appears to have been a substantial shift from usership to private ownership (Table 4.7). This conclusion is highly uncertain, however, because the proportions in 1992 and 1994 are calculated on a different base: the 1992 figures are percent of number of parcels in each tenure category, while the 1994 figures are percent of hectares in each category.

Employee households identified the village council as the main source of land (almost 85% of the land in an average plot), while the collective farm was the source for about 15% of the land in an average household plot (Table 4.7).

Table 4.7. Land Tenure and Sources of Land in Household Plots*

	1994	1992
Tenure:		
Private ownership	45.1	30.3
Lifetime possession	16.8	13.1
Usership	38.0	55.8
Lease	0.1	0.8
Sources:		
District council	1.8	1.9
Village council	83.3	62.5
Farm enterprise	14.7	35.0
Other	0.2	0.7

* Figures for 1994 are percent of total plot area; figures for 1992 are percent of total number of parcels held by each household.

Only half the respondents reported having a document that attests to their rights to use the household plot. Respondents with documents have significantly larger plots than the rest, and they also have a much greater area in private ownership (Table 4.8). In this group of respondents, fully 40% own their entire plot (compared to the sample average rate of 25%), and only 30% do not have any privately owned land (compared to the sample average rate of 60%). Both households with documents and those without reported relatively high confidence that the family will keep the plot in the future: 75% of families with documents are confident that they will keep the plot compared to 62% of families without any documents.

Table 4.8. Average Size and Composition of a Household Plot (hundredths of ha)

	All sample	Respondents*	
		with documents	without documents
Total plot	33	43	23
Privately owned	15	25	4
Lifetime possession	6	7	3
Usership	13	10	15
Leased	0.1	0.0	0.2

* Respondents with documents are 51% of the sample; respondents without documents are 49%.

Despite the small size of the household plots in the sample, two-thirds of the employees reported that they do not wish to expand their plots. Those who do wish to enlarge their household plots have fairly modest objectives: an average increase of less than 0.5 ha. There is no significant difference in plot size reported between individuals who wish to enlarge their plots and those who do not wish to expand (about 0.3 ha in both groups).

Around 80% of employees reported that they pay a land tax, but the reported tax payments vary so greatly that either respondents or enumerators were probably unclear about units of reporting for tax purposes. Among the very few (2% of respondents) who reported that they lease some land, lease payments were reported to be on the same order of magnitude as the land tax.

Two-thirds of the employees have a negative attitude toward the decision to allow buying and selling of land in Russia. Moreover, fully 40% of the employees are of the opinion that land in subsidiary household plots should be in the traditional form of inheritable lifetime possession. Yet another 40% support private ownership for household land with the right to sell. Both the usership proponents and the private ownership proponents are equally represented among the respondents who are opposed to buying and selling of land in Russia. Respondents thus appear to differentiate household land from commercial agricultural land, and are more supportive of market transactions in household land.

Attitude Toward Private Farming

Farm employees are the natural cadre from which private farmers can emerge. However, over 90% of the employees in the sample reported that they do not intend to become private farmers within the next 2-3 years. This is a higher proportion than in the previous survey (85%). The difference is statistically significant, and although the results are based on unmatched samples from the two surveys they seem to indicate increased disillusionment with the prospects of private farming among the employees of farm enterprises in the sample provinces.

Table 4.9. Views of Private Farming Expressed by Members and Employees of Farm Enterprises

Why Not Become a Private Farmer? Main reasons cited by those who do not intend to become private farmers*	1994	1992
Insufficient capital	74	62
Difficulties with farm inputs	60	65
Afraid of risk	56	41
No wish to change life style	42	31
No full legal guarantees	40	36
Reasons of age and health	29	25
More stable income in collective	27	15
No economic and legal skills	25	17
Family does not want to farm	20	18
Afraid to lose social benefits	19	18
Higher income in collective	17	11
Inadequate land	15	17
Negative attitude in the village	11	2
Restrictions on buying/selling of land	6	12

* In 1994, 92% of respondents reported that they did not intend to become farmers; in 1992, the corresponding proportion of respondents was 85%.

The main factors that are perceived as obstacles to becoming a private farmer are insufficient capital (74% of respondents), difficulties with purchase of machinery and equipment (60%), and risk aversion (56%). Other factors reported by around 40% of respondents

include reluctance to change the life style and lack of legal guarantees. As in the previous survey, potential loss of social benefits and services, inadequate skills, and poor quality of land allocated to private farmers are not reported to be serious deterrents (Table 4.9). The ranking of perceived obstacles to private farming is on the whole identical in both surveys.

While 55% of the employees support the right of individuals to receive land for private farming, more than 35% are opposed. Even among those who favor private ownership of subsidiary household plots (see previous section), only 40% support private ownership of land in private farms. Farm employees reported varying opinions about the desirable form of tenure for land in private farms, with approximately equal support for long-term lease from the state, lifetime inheritable possession, and private ownership with the right to sell.

Household Production: Livestock and Crops

Employees reported spending nearly 5 hours a day tending the household plot during the summer months and 3 hours a day during the winter. In addition, employees reported working 8-hour working days at the farm enterprise (10-hour working days during 5-6 months of the peak season).

Most households (over 85%) produce potatoes, vegetables, and meat (Table 4.10). Milk and eggs are produced by around 60% of households. Very few households produce grain (around 5%), and virtually none produce technical crops, such as sugar beet or oilseeds. Most households reported intentions to keep the same commodity mix in the future (Table 4.10). There is, however, a reported tendency to increase livestock production, particularly meat.

With access to very little land, households continue to specialize in livestock production. Practically all households in the sample reported keeping some livestock. Around 80% of households keep cattle (bulls, cows, and young animals in various proportions) and 75% keep pigs and piglets (Table 4.11). An average household with cattle has

2.6 head, including 1.2 cows, 0.7 young animals (under 1 year), 0.3 bulls, and 0.4 heifers (under 2 years). The number of cows reported per household ranged from 1 to 4, with an average of 1.3. The average number of bulls, heifers, and calves was less than 1.5 per household reporting keeping these animals. Households with pigs reported between 1 and 10 animals, with an average of 1.8. The number of chickens ranged from 1 to 60, with an average of 17 birds per households (Table 4.11).

Table 4.10. Production in Household Plots

	Percent of producers	Quantity produced, kg*	Plans for 1994#	
			up	unchanged
Grain	6	1600	3	67
Potatoes	94	1700	15	81
Vegetable	87	330	16	83
Fruits	39	190	10	74
Meat	86	320	31	62
Milk	61	3750	18	72
Eggs	63	1950	23	69
Wool	20	12	4	71

* Average quantity per household produced in 1993.
\# Percent of respondents.

Table 4.11. Livestock in Households (average per household)

	Percent of households	Number of animals
Cattle	79	2.6
Cows	74	1.3
Pigs	55	1.8
Piglets	33	2.6
Chickens	83	16.8
Sheep	23	5.2
Rabbits	8	6.3

The average milk yield in household farms in the sample was reported at approximately 3200 kg per cow per year. This is nearly 45% higher than yields in the farm enterprises, which average around 2200 kg per cow per year. Egg yields are low, however, at under 200 eggs per year.

Nearly 80% of households have access to common pasture. Over 40% of households produce all their hay needs, but only 20% of households report that they are self-sufficient in concentrated feed. Nearly half the households reported producing up to 25% of their concentrated feed and a quarter produce up to 25% of their hay needs.

Household farmers were on the whole satisfied with the profitability of livestock production. Over 80% of producers report that milk, pork, poultry, and eggs are profitable; beef is reported to be profitable by 60% of households and wool by 50%.

Marketing

Although respondents reported that most of production from the household plot is consumed by the family, some is sold commercially. Over half the producers in the sample reported selling meat and milk (Table 4.12). Meat is the main commercial product of households: nearly 30% of meat produced is sold. Milk, wool, and grain are also sold in substantial quantities outside the household (around 15% of production). Crop products other than grain are mostly consumed within the family. Households reporting commercial sales have a significantly larger volume of production than the average for all producers in the sample (Table 4.12).

Livestock products account for 86% of income from commercial sales of households, and crop products account for 14%. Livestock products are the only source of commercial income from the plot in 70% of households. This distribution of income from commercial sales emphasizes the dichotomy between livestock and crop products for households: the former (meat, milk, eggs, wool) are sold commercially in significant quantities, while the latter (potatoes, vegetables, fruits) are produced for own consumption.

Farmers' markets provide the main outlet for commercial sales of household production. Farmers' markets are identified by over 40% of respondents as the main marketing channel for meat, by over 50% as the main channel for milk, fruits, and vegetables, and by nearly 90% as the main sales channel for eggs (Table 4.13). State procurement is the main channel for 30% of potato and vegetable growers and for 25% of meat producers. The local collective farm is the main sales channel for most grain producers (67%) and for 25% of milk producers. Most respondents reported that they can choose a buyer for their products and that they are not constrained to sell through a particular channel (Table 4.13).

The prices received by households are reported to be approximately the same as prices reported by managers of farm enterprises (Table 4.14). The prices received for meat, the main commercial product of household plots, are in fact significantly higher, as households sell their meat mostly through farmers' markets, while farm enterprises deliver the product to the state-controlled regional meat processor. Prices received for grain appear to be the only exception, as the few households that do sell grain deliver it mainly to the local farm enterprise, which naturally pays them below the price that it in turn receives from state procurement channels. The prices for grain received by households are indeed significantly lower than those received by farm enterprises (Table 4.14).

Table 4.12. Employees Reporting Production and Commercial Sales by Product

	Percent of producers in sample	Percent of producers reporting sales	Average output, kg/year		Percent of output sold	
			all producers	commercial producers	all producers	commercial producers
Grain	6	21	1600	2300	17	83
Potatoes	94	17	1700	3200	7	43
Vegetables	87	1	330	500	0	20
Fruits	39	3	190	530	1	51
Meat	86	51	320	460	28	55
Milk	61	52	3750	4850	15	41
Eggs (pcs)	63	7	1951	3300	2	35
Wool	20	18	12	24	15	82

Table 4.13. Marketing Channels for Household Plots (percent of respondents)

	Main channel				Can choose buyer
	Farmers' market	Procurement organizations	Collective farm	Commercial firms	
Grain	17	17	67	--	83
Potatoes	33	44	3	14	68
Vegetables	50	33	--	--	67
Fruits	67	--	--	--	33
Meat	43	30	8	16	80
Milk	59	6	25	--	57
Eggs	87	4	--	--	65
Wool	44	22	17	--	39

Table 4.14. Prices Received by Households and Farm Enterprises (rubles per kg)

	Months of sale in 1993	Average price received	
		Farm enterprises	*Households*
Meat	Nov-Dec	812	1345*
Milk	Nov-Dec	148	143
Eggs	Dec	72	386
Wool	Dec	397	1505
Potatoes	Sep-Oct	67	63
Grain	Aug-Oct	59	47*

* Average prices significantly different between farm enterprises and households.

Social Services and Expectations

Although employees continue to enjoy a wide range of social services that are traditionally provided by the farm enterprise, the level of provision of many services in 1994 was lower than in 1992 (Table 4.15). The reported decline is not restricted to services and benefits provided exclusively by the farm enterprise, such as transport, house maintenance, and subsidized rent and repairs. It is also noticeable for state-funded services and benefits, such as medical care and child allowances. The general pattern of social services in 1994 compared to 1992 as reported by employees is similar to that reported by farm managers (Table 4.15).

There is a striking difference in the evaluation of the reform process by employees and private farmers. The employees on the whole are much more pessimistic than the farmers. Nearly 70% of employees reported that the material situation of their families had deteriorated during the last 2-3 years (Fig. 4.2), and 40% of respondents reported that the deterioration had been substantial. The difficult situation of the employees is demonstrated by the answers on the purchasing power of their cash income (Fig. 4.3): 20% reported that the cash income is insufficient for subsistence and 50% reported that it is just sufficient for subsistence needs. Only a quarter of the respondents indicated

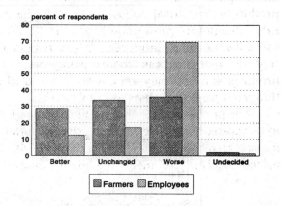

Fig. 4.2. How Has the Family Situation Changed?

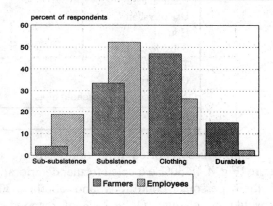

Fig. 4.3. What the Family Budget Buys

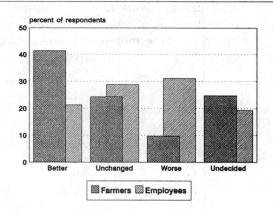

Fig. 4.4. Perception of Family Future

that enough is left from their cash income after satisfying subsistence needs in order to buy clothing and other necessities. Virtually no one reported ability to afford furniture, durable consumer goods, and other "luxuries."

Table 4.15. Reported Availability of Social Services and Benefits (percent of respondents)

	Farm Managers		Farm Employees	
	1992	*1994*	*1992*	*1994*
Compensation for price increases	40.0	26.5	24.4	13.4
Pension augmentation	21.2	4.7	8.3	2.4
Child allowances	50.4	41.9	38.1	13.6
Day care	79.2	63.7	--	13.2
School subsidies	70.8	61.5	--	23.9
Student stipends	82.7	75.2	7.2	4.1
House maintenance and repairs	91.5	83.8	40.8	26.4
Heating fuel	76.5	57.3	--	20.7
Subsidized food	88.1	91.5	63.9	62.5
Subsidized consumer goods	21.2	27.8	14.7	5.5
Subsidized utilities	69.2	55.6	--	16.0
Medical care	69.2	68.4	82.9	51.3
Use of vacation facilities	82.3	76.5	32.3	20.5
Housing	72.7	53.8	--	24.5
Subsidized rent	52.3	39.3	20.8	14.4
Transport	95.4	96.6	84.6	72.0
Other services	5.0	--	0.4	--
Assistance with household plots	--		67.3	
Number of respondents	260	234	1427	507

Employees reported little optimism for the future (Fig. 4.4): 30% expected further deterioration of their personal conditions and another 30% expected no change. Only 20% of respondents anticipate some improvement.

In all cases, private farmers reported more positive evaluations of their family situation and more optimistic expectations of future prospects. For nearly 70% of private farmers the family situation had not deteriorated, and 30% actually reported an improvement (Fig. 4.2). Over 60% of the farmers earn more than what is needed for subsistence, and nearly 20% can even afford "luxuries," including vehicles (Fig. 4.3). Nearly 70% of private farmers do not anticipate deterioration of family fortunes in the immediate future, and fully 40% are optimistic (Fig. 4.4).

5. Private Farmers

The emergence of private farming outside the scope of large-scale collective farms is perhaps the most tangible manifestation of the process of land reform in Russia. While many of the private farmers are former employees of farm enterprises, they pursue a farming strategy which is distinctly different from that of household plots. Private farmers emphasize production of crops instead of livestock, and produce primarily for commercial purposes. Their allotments span tens of hectares, and although not all of it is privately owned land at this stage, the size appears to be sufficient for profitable small-scale commercial farming.

Demographic Profile

The average size of a private farmer's household is 3.8 persons, with 80% of the families in the range between 3 and 5 persons. The head of household is on average 40 years old, and the spouse is 38. Nearly 40% of family members in the sample are children and young people under 20. The number of older people over 60 in the sample is 4%. The family size and age characteristics of private farmer households are virtually identical to those of farm employee households. This is understandable, because three-quarters of private farmers are former employees of collective and state farms.

Over 70% of the private farmers in the sample have lived all their lives in the rural area and another 8% have lived there for more than 10 years. Mobility of the rural population is very low: 65% of the respondents have lived in the same village for more than 10 years. Although most private farmers are rural residents, fully 13% of the respondents report that they live in town.

Three-quarters of the respondents had worked as managers, specialists, or skilled workers on collective and state farms before they became private farmers. Another 15% had worked in industrial enterprises and 5% had held jobs in the social sphere. The number of former government officials in the sample is less than 3%. The respondents had mainly worked in the local village or in the adjacent rural areas. Only 12% had worked in town.

Although private farmers are largely former farm employees, the prospect of private farming appeals only to a select subpopulation. Private farmers in the sample are better educated than farm employees (Table 5.1). Twenty-three percent of the private farmers have higher education, compared to 17% of farm employees in the sample. The proportion of private farmers and their spouses reporting fewer than 9 grades of schooling is significantly lower than among farm employees.

Table 5.1. Education Profile of Private Farmers and Farm Employees (percent of respondents)

	Farmers		Employees	
	Head of Household	Spouse	Head of Household	Spouse
Higher education	23	18	17	12
Secondary education	65	71	60	65
Uncompleted secondary (8 grades or less)	11	11	19	21
Professional courses	1	1	3	1
Illiterate	0	0	0	0
Number of persons	1030	1025	507	497

Table 5.2. Housing of Private Farmers

	Percent of respondents	Ownership		
		Family	Farm enterprise	Village council
Separate house	60	90	7	0
Apartment				
in a small building	28	71	24	3
in a large block	11	39	13	29
All sample	**100**	**78**	**13**	**4**

Sixty percent of private farmers in the sample live in separate houses, and the remaining 40% report that they live in apartments. The housing is mostly privately owned (80% of respondents), but 12.5% live in housing owned by a farm enterprise (Table 5.2). Another 4% live in housing owned by the village council. When ownership is analyzed by type of housing, the responses indicate that fully 90% of separate houses are privately owned, while a quarter of the apartments in small buildings are owned by the farm enterprise and more than a quarter of the apartments in large blocks are owned by the village council.

The housing is typically equipped with electricity (94% of respondents), but running water is fully available only in half the dwellings. Farm structures are connected to electricity in 60% of the cases and only 10% have full running water. Access roads, while not a problem for residential housing, are not available for one third of farm structures; some 40% of farm structures have full access roads and another 20% report partial access.

Farm Size and Ownership

Even the smallest private farms are significantly larger than the household plots in the sample. There are no farms smaller than 2 ha, and only 1% of farms in the sample are smaller than 5 ha, whereas the average household plot is less than 0.5 ha. One quarter of the farms in the sample have between 25 ha and 50 ha of land, and the median farm size is 54 ha (Fig. 5.1). Most of the land in an average farm (85%) is arable. In Orlov, Rostov, and Saratov arable land accounts for more than 90% of the average farm, whereas in Novosibirsk and Pskov, where livestock production is relatively important, arable land is between 60%-70%, with 20%-30% in hayland and pasture (Table 5.3).

While the median farm size in the sample is 54 ha, the average is 90 ha (Table 5.3). The relatively large average size is attributable to the presence of 14 farms in the sample (1.4% of respondents) that report over 500 ha of land. The reported farm sizes in this upper tail of the distribution range up to 3438 ha. The very large farms are all concentrated in Saratov Province, where the average farm size is 155 ha. Outside of Saratov, the largest farms (89 ha on average) are reported in Novosibirsk Province in Western Siberia, where farm sizes range from 7.4 ha to 366 ha. Pskov Province has the smallest farms (less than 20 ha on average).

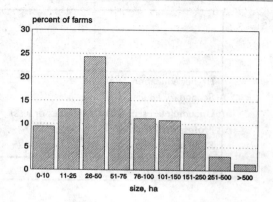

Fig. 5.1. Size Distribution of Private Farms

The unusually large size of private farms in Saratov is attributable to the special organization of private farming in this province. While most private farms in the sample (86%) are one- and two-family farms, there is a group of multiple-family farms in Saratov (3% of the sample) that include 10-50 families, with as many as 90 families per farm in one case. The average number of families per farm in all the provinces except Saratov is 1.2-1.6, while the farms in Saratov include on average 4.3 families (Table 5.4). Each family contributes its allotment of land to the "composite" farm. There is a very strong correlation (0.86) between farm size and the number of families constituting the farm. While one- and two-family farms average 60-70 ha, farms constituted by more than 10 families are 750 ha on average (Table 5.5). When adjusted for the number of families, the area of farmland per family is about 50 ha.

Table 5.3. Average Size of Private Farms and Structure of Land Use

	Number of farms	Farm size, ha	Structure of land use, in percent of farm size					
			Arable	Orchards	Hayland	Pasture	Forest	Other
All sample	**1030**	**89.8**	**86.0**	**0.1**	**5.5**	**6.0**	**0.9**	**1.6**
Novosibirsk	250	89.0	63.8	0.1	19.0	10.7	3.0	3.4
Orel	177	73.2	91.0	0.3	2.6	3.0	0.8	2.2
Pskov	130	17.5	68.1	0.6	13.2	7.4	0.6	10.2
Rostov	200	63.2	94.5	0.1	0.2	4.7	0.3	0.3
Saratov	273	155.2	94.6	0.0	0.4	4.7	0.0	0.4

Table 5.4. Distribution of Number of Households per Private Farm (in percent)

Number of households	All sample	Novo-sibirsk	Orel	Pskov	Rostov	Saratov
1	**69.6**	75.2	80.5	84.6	70.8	49.5
2	**16**	13	13.2	13.9	14.9	22.3
3-5	**9.1**	8.5	5.8	1.5	12.8	12.8
6-9	**2.6**	3.3	--	--	1	5.9
10-90	**2.8**	--	0.6	--	0.5	9.5
Average number of households	**2.2**	1.5	1.3	1.2	1.6	4.3

Half the farmland is reported to be in private ownership and another quarter is leased (Fig. 5.2, Table 5.6). In the previous survey conducted in 1992, about half of land parcels in private farms were privately owned, just over a quarter were in lifetime possession, and 17% were leased. There has been no change in the proportion of privately owned land since 1992, but the importance of leasing in the sample has increased, while that of lifetime possession and usership declined. Mid-sized farms are more active in leasing markets than are large farms. Farms of between 50 ha and 250 ha on average lease 30% of their land, while the proportion of leased land in farms larger than 500 ha is less than 10%. The very large farms correspondingly have a high proportion of privately owned land, 50-70%, comparable to the proportion of privately owned land in small farms with up to

50 ha. Medium-sized farms of 50-250 ha own about 40% of their land. The pattern of ownership and leasing reflects the process of formation of large and medium sized farms. Large farms are amalgamations of many family allotments, each averaging about 40 ha. Medium-sized farms are in general formed from one or two allotments, and the remainder of the land is leased in.

The private farmers report on average that half their land was received from the district council and the other half from the local collective enterprise (Table 5.7). The collective farm enterprise is a source of land only for former farm employees (75% of the respondents). On exit, they received on average 30 ha of land, which represents the combined entitlement of a husband-and-wife couple (farm managers report 12 ha as the average land share of farm employees). While former farm employees received 60% of their land from the

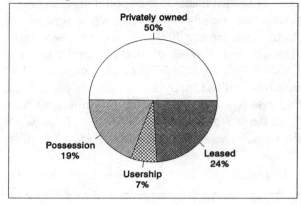

Fig. 5.2. Land Tenure in Private Farms

farm enterprise, all other farmers (former industrial workers, employees in the social sphere, etc.) received virtually their entire allotment from the district council.

Table 5.5. Average Size of Single-Family and Multi-Family Farms (in hectares)

	Average for all families	*Single-family farms*	*Multi-family farms*				
			2	*3-5*	*6-9*	*10-90*	*all*
All sample	**89.8**	**61.1**	**68.3**	**112.6**	**222.7**	**750.2**	**156.1**
Novosibirsk	89.0	91.9	85.7	86.7	32.1	--	79.0
Orel	73.2	66.8	70.1	185.1	--	--	101.9
Pskov	17.4	16.8	20.8	26.1	--	--	21.3
Rostov	63.2	56.9	58.0	99.2	105.5	121.3	78.9
Saratov	155.2	53.2	77.3	232.8	322.6	803.1	254.9

Table 5.6. Structure of Land Tenure in Private Farms (in percent of farm size)

	Number of farms	*Farm size, ha*	*Private land*	*Lifetime possession*	*Usership*	*Lease*
All sample	**1030**	**89.8**	**49.9**	**19.5**	**6.6**	**24.1**
Novosibirsk	250	89.0	39.7	20.6	14.6	25.1
Orel	177	73.2	13.8	39.4	12.3	34.5
Pskov	130	17.5	73.1	12.8	0.3	13.7
Rostov	200	63.2	36.6	24.9	3.0	35.5
Saratov	273	155.2	68.9	11.6	2.0	17.5

Table 5.7. Sources of Land in Private Farms by Province (in percent of farm size)

	Number of farms	Farm size, ha	District council	Village council	Farm enterprise	Other enterprises	Private individuals
All sample	**1030**	**89.8**	**48.8**	**1.7**	**47.8**	**0.5**	**1.2**
Novosibirsk	250	89.0	69.3	0.8	27.8	0.2	2.0
Orel	177	73.2	87.0	4.7	7.3	0.7	0.2
Pskov	130	17.5	71.5	3.5	24.7	0.0	0.3
Rostov	200	63.2	54.4	2.8	40.5	0.3	2.0
Saratov	273	155.2	23.4	0.8	74.1	0.8	1.0

Table 5.8. Preferred Form of Land Tenure in Private Farms and Household Plots as Reported by Private Farmers, Farm-Enterprise Employees, and Managers (percent of respondents)

	Land in private farms			Land in household plots	
	Private farmers	Employees	Managers	Employees	Managers
Long-term lease from the state	4.1	19.7	25.6	8.9	14.1
Lifetime inheritable possession	24.7	20.3	39.3	38.3	41.0
Private ownership	66.2	15.8	18.8	41.6	38.9
Undecided	5.0	44.2	16.3	11.2	6.0

Attitude toward Ownership of Land

Private farmers are predominantly in favor of private ownership of land. Two thirds of the respondents reported that private farmers should own their land (Table 5.8). This is in striking contrast to the views of farm-enterprise employees and managers, among whom fewer than 20% accept private ownership of land by farmers, although 40% of the same group of respondents are in favor of privately owned land in household plots. A similar polarization is observed in the reported attitude to buying and selling of land. While over 50% of private farmers support the right to buy and sell land, only 15% of farm-enterprise managers and employees share this opinion (Table 5.9).

Attitudes of private farmers and other rural residents thus differ markedly with regard to the desirability of allowing land markets to function. Land markets appear to be understood by many purely as a venue for speculative activity. The rural population still does not recognize the role of land markets as a vehicle for preserving the value of land and increasing its productivity by providing a medium for transfer of land from less efficient to more efficient producers and creation of farms of optimal size.

Table 5.9. Attitude to Buy-and-Sell Transactions in Land among Private Farmers, Farm-Enterprise Employees, and Managers (percent of respondents)

	Positive	Negative	Undecided
Private farmers	52.7	36.9	10.4
Employees	14.7	79.1	6.1
Managers	15.4	79.5	5.1

Family Income

Private farmers in the sample are commercial producers, and rely on farming as their primary source of livelihood. Half the private farmers report that over 75% of their family income is derived from the farm. Private farmers differ significantly from farm employees in their sources of family income. Although earnings from household plots are important to farm employees, employees in the sample reported that on average 25% of family income derived from the household plots, and the remainder from wages and salaries (Fig. 5.3).

Fig. 5.3. Farm Income: Private Farmers and Employees

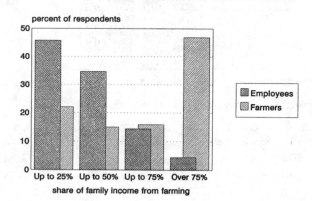

Households of private farmers also diversify their sources of income to supplement earnings and to insure against the uncertainties and risks of farming. While the head of the household devotes his entire time to the farm, the spouse in half of cases works outside the farm, earning a supplementary income independent of the fortunes of the private farm (Table 5.10).

Production

Private farmers specialize in crop production to a greater extent than do large-scale collective enterprises and employee households. Virtually all private farmers report that they produce crops, and only 50% report livestock production. Pure livestock farms apparently do not exist, and farms with livestock also produce crops. This is in striking contrast to household plots, in 70% of which all sales derive entirely from livestock products.

Table 5.10. Employment of Head of Household and Spouse in Private-Farmer Families

Main Occupation	1994	1992
Head of household		
Private farm	96.5	93.5
Spouse		
Private farm	50.5	43.5
Local farm enterprise	17.5	19.6
Social sphere in the village	13.6	15.1
Other enterprise	6.0	7.3
Housekeeping	5.7	7.4
Employment on Farm		*1992*
Head of household		
full time on farm		95.0
Spouse		
full time on farm		44.2
part time on farm		35.8
not working on farm		17.0

The main crop products on private farms in the sample are grain (produced by more than 90% of farms) and potatoes and vegetables (produced by half the farms in the sample). The product composition of the private sector reflects the importance of the grain belt in the geography of the sample. Although the private sector in aggregate produces 10% of Russian sunflower (see Table 1.3 in Chapter 1), sunflower production is not very prominent on private farms in this sample (Table 5.11). Sugar beet, another popular technical crop in Russia, is produced by fewer than 3% of private farms in the sample. The production volume of private farms is substantially greater than that of household plots (Table 5.11). Their specialization is also different: potatoes, vegetables, and livestock products, the traditional output of household plots, are less popular among private farms in the sample.

In mixed crop/livestock farms, cash crops as well as feed are grown on the arable land. Even farms relatively specialized in livestock derive only half their farm income from livestock products, and the remaining half comes from sales of crop products. In the entire sample of private farmers 25% of farm income is attributed to livestock sales and 70% is derived from crop production. These figures are radically different from the production pattern of employee households, where on average 86% of income derives from livestock sales and only 14% from crops. The product mix in large-scale farm enterprises is also different from that in private farms: incomes on large farms are equally divided between crops and livestock (Fig. 5.4).

Although only 50% of farmers report that they engage in livestock production, as many as 60% keep cattle (Table 5.12) and produce meat and milk (Table 5.11). Those who identify themselves as livestock producers have more animals and higher volume of production than the remainder, for whom production is intended largely for home consumption. Virtually all livestock producers grow their own hay (94% of respondents) and many make their own concentrated feed (83%).

Most producers report that livestock production is profitable at their chosen levels and technology of production. Some 60% of private

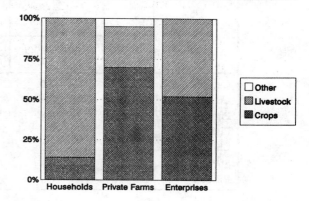

Fig. 5.4. Product Mix in Different Farm Categories

producers of milk, beef, and pork report that production is profitable, as do 90% of producers of eggs and poultry. In contrast, most managers of large-scale farms report that livestock production is not profitable in their enterprises (similarly to the 1992 survey).

Table 5.11. Production of Private Farms and Household Plots (average quantity per farm/household produced in 1993)

	Private farms		Household plots		Plans for 1994 (percent of farmers)		
	Percent of producers	Quantity, ton	Percent of producers	Quantity, ton	up	down	unchanged
Grain	87	99.5	6	1.6	19	12	64
Potatoes	45	8.6	94	1.7	4	3	91
Vegetables	41	3.5	87	0.3	3	0	96
Fruits	13	1.2	39	0.2	1	0	96
Sunflower	18	26.6	--	--	9	7	79
Hay	31	114.6	--	--	5	4	89
Beef	50	1.5	86	0.3	18	10	70
Pork	51	6.2	(including pork & poultry)		18	5	74
Milk	60	8.5	61	3.8	14	5	78
Poultry	31	0.4	NA	NA	10	0	88
Eggs (thou.)	45	49.2	63	2.0	11	0	88
Wool	23	0.13	20	0.01	3	4	91

Table 5.12. Livestock in Private Farms and Household Plots (average per household)

	Private Farms		Private Farms Identified as Livestock Producers		Household Plots	
	Percent of farms	*Number of animals*	*Percent of farms*	*Number of animals*	*Percent of households*	*Number of animals*
Cattle	62	7.0	46	8.3	79	2.6
Cows	60	3.2	45	3.7	74	1.3
Pigs	39	4.0	28	4.5	55	1.8
Piglets	25	5.4	20	6.1	33	2.6
Chickens	51	33.9	37	38.0	83	16.8
Sheep	28	16.1	23	18.3	23	5.2
Rabbits	4	10.5	3	11.1	8	6.3

Labor and Machinery

A private farm in the sample employs on average 4 people, of whom 2 are members of the immediate family and 1.6 are members of the extended family (relatives and members of other families constituting the farm). The remaining 0.4 workers are hired help, mostly seasonal. Private farms employ very little permanent hired help (on average 0.1 person per farm). Only 4% of farms report hiring permanent help and 10% hire temporary help during seasonal peaks. These results are consistent with the findings of the 1992 survey that private farms rely largely on family labor. Around 40% of farms employ 1-2 workers, and fewer than 5% of farms employ more than 10 workers (Fig. 5.5). Only 1.2% of farms employ more than 20 workers.

Multi-family farms employ on average twice as many workers as single-family farms, while their average size is 2.5 times as large (Table 5.13). The ratio of labor to land is thus slightly lower in multi-family farms. Immediate family of farm members account for 80% of the total number of employed in multi-family farms, whereas in single-family farms household members represent only 66% of all labor (Table 5.13). Regression analysis indicates that each additional family in a multi-family farm contributes less than one (0.71) additional workers. Multi-family farms thus appear to include more part-time workers and perhaps pensioners among their member families than do single family private farms.

In both single- and multiple-family farms, the land endowment is around 26 ha per worker. This is virtually identical to the land endowment per worker in the large-scale farm enterprises when the full labor force is taken into account (including nonagricultural labor and those employed in the social sphere). If only agricultural labor is taken into consideration, farm enterprises report lower labor intensity than private farms (38 ha per agricultural worker). The finding that crop-growing private farms are more labor intensive are more labor intensive than traditional collectives suggests that private farmers use production technologies

Fig. 5.5. Number of Employed in Private Farms

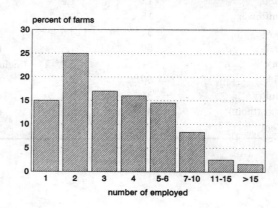

reflecting low costs of labor and high costs of capital. Private farms rely much less on livestock than the large enterprises, and their higher labor intensity is probably due to their limited stock of farm equipment. The data on labor intensity suggest that transition from large-scale farm enterprises to family farms will not necessarily result in massive rural unemployment, as is often feared in Russia.

Table 5.13. Farm Labor and Farm Size Indicators

	All sample	Single-family farms	Multi-family farms
Number of employed	**4.1**	**3.2**	**6.3**
Family members	2.1	2.1	2.1
From other households	1.0	0.1	2.9
Permanent hired labor	0.1	0.1	0.1
Seasonal hired labor	0.3	0.3	0.4
Relatives/friends	0.6	0.6	0.8
Number of families	**2.2**	**1.0**	**4.9**
Size, hectares	**90**	**61**	**156**

Table 5.14. Farmers with Agricultural Machinery

Machine	Percent of owners	Average number per farm reporting the machine
Tractors	78	1.8
Mini-tractors	3	1.3
Trucks	52	1.3
Plows	60	1.4
Seeders	52	1.6
Hay mowers	23	1.1
Harvesters	27	1.4
Grain combines	37	1.2
Potato combines	2	1.1
Potato diggers	6	1.2
Milking machines	6	1.5
Other machines	48	3.9

Most private farms have some machinery. Among the farms that report their equipment inventory (87% of respondents), an average farm

has 8 pieces of diverse equipment. The most commonly owned machines are tractors (full-scale, not mini), trucks, plows, and seeders (Table 5.14). On average, the farms have one tractor per 30 ha of land and one truck per 45 ha.

Marketing

Private farms have a definite commercial orientation, although they also produce for family consumption. The main cash products are grain, sunflower, meat, and milk (Table 5.15). More than two-thirds of grain output and nearly half the meat is sold commercially. Although sunflower is produced by a relatively small proportion of farms in the sample, most of the output is also sold commercially. Other commercial products are wool and sugar beet, although again the number of producers in these categories is small. The traditional household-plot products, such as potatoes, vegetables, fruits and berries, and eggs, are mainly consumed by the family and a very small proportion of the output is sold commercially. The commodity composition of sales does not differ much from that observed in the 1992 survey.

Table 5.15. Proportion of Output Consumed and Sold by Private Farmers

Commodity	Producers in the sample, %	Percentage of output	
		Consumed	Sold
Grain	91	31	69
Sugar beet	2	40	60
Sunflower	18	9	91
Potatoes	51	94	6
Vegetables	48	97	3
Fruits&berries	18	98	2
Meat	61	57	43
Milk	59	71	29
Eggs	44	97	3
Wool	24	70	30

Farmers sell most products, except grain, sunflower, and sugar beet, both to state procurement channels and directly to consumers (Table 5.16), with sales to the local collective enterprise or other commercial structures ranking a relatively distant third. Sales to procurement organizations dominated marketing in early 1994, but their weight declined to some extent compared with the 1992 survey. The change in marketing patterns is consistent with national trends reported in Table 1.12 (see Chapter 1). The volume of direct sales to consumers increased in the 1994 sample relative to 1992.

Farmers reported that, despite the dominance of traditional procurement organizations, they were reasonably able to choose the buyer for their products. Even in state monopolized products such as grain, sunflower, and sugar beet, 30%-50% of farmers stated that they could find alternative marketing channels if necessary (Table 5.15).

Table 5.16. Main Marketing Channels by Commodity (percent of private farmers selling the commodity)

Commodity	Number of farmers reporting sales	Procurement organizations	Collective farms and other enterprises	Direct sales	Choice of buyer available
Commodities sold by more than 15 percent of private farms:					
Grain	800	90	8	2	34
Meat	452	46	11	42	75
Milk	317	25	27	47	38
Sunflower	176	68	25	6	55
Commodities sold by fewer than 10 percent of private farms:					
Wool	89	64	3	17	26
Potatoes	60	47	23	28	52
Vegetables	20	45	10	40	95
Eggs	26	4	4	92	62
Sugar beet	13	85	--	8	31
Fruits&berries	7	14	--	86	71

Farmers report that prices received for their products are too low (Table 5.17). This complaint applies to all products, regardless of the main marketing channel. Late payments are a substantial problem mainly for products sold through state channels, such as grain, sunflower, and wool. Roughly half of farmers report difficulties finding a buyer for their products. This is not entirely consistent with the finding in Table 5.16, where a relatively high percentage of farmers reported that they had a choice of buyers, but the availability of buyers was probably interpreted differently by the respondents in the two questions. Both late payments and the ability to find a buyer appear to have become worse compared to the 1992 survey. This observation is consistent with the aggregate data reported in Chapter 1 indicating that the payment period for agricultural producers lengthened in 1994. Both the sample and the aggregate data suggest that late payment is a worsening problem.

Despite the persistent reports of low prices, there is no evidence of discrimination in pricing against private farmers. Prices received by private farmers are comparable to those received by farm enterprises (Table 5.18). Fewer than 40% of farmers feel that they face more difficult marketing conditions than collective farms in the area.

Table 5.17. Marketing Problems as Reported by Private Farmers
(percent of total number of producers selling in each commodity category)

Commodity	Number of sellers	Reported problems				
		Late payment	Low price	No buyer	Transport	Other
Grain	800	87	92	65	30	6
Meat	452	31	75	39	26	3
Milk	317	51	87	58	31	3
Sunflower	176	64	86	48	14	1
Wool	89	29	75	57	12	--
Potatoes	60	25	70	53	27	2
Eggs	26	--	15	19	12	--
Vegetables	20	35	55	50	20	--
Sugar beet	13	23	39	23	15	15
Fruits&berries	7	14	43	29	71	--

Table 5.18. Prices Received by Farm Enterprises, Households, and Private Farmers (rubles/kg)

	Months of sale in 1993	Average price received		
		Farm enterprises	Household plots	Private farms
Meat	Nov-Dec	812	1345	1270
Milk	Nov-Dec	148	143	135
Eggs	Dec	72	386	--
Wool	Dec	397	1505	530
Potatoes	Sep-Oct	67	63	102
Grain	Aug-Oct	59	47	60
Sunflower	Oct-Dec	114	--	110

Farm Inputs

Traditional organizations in the former state supply system remain the main source of farm inputs for private farmers (Table 5.19). Farmers turn to the local farm enterprise for seeds and seedlings, farm machinery, spare parts, mechanized field services, and veterinary medicine (including drugs). Private sources (including farmers cooperatives) still play a relatively minor role as input suppliers, but they provide professional consulting, supplementing state research stations and the specialists of the local collective farm. The overall pattern of supply channels remains the same as in the 1992 survey, indicating that there has been little progress over the intervening two years in improving provision of inputs and services on a commercial and competitive basis.

Although the private sector is insufficiently developed in rural Russia to provide many of the needs of private farmers, an increasing percentage of farmers report that they sell farm inputs to others in the area. The last column in Table 5.19 presents the proportion of private farmers in the sample who report that they sell various farm inputs and services to other users. Most frequently farmers sell machinery services, but they also report selling fuel to their neighbors in small quantities. Private farmers also sell consulting services and seeds and seedlings. The percentage of private farmers acting as suppliers of inputs and services on the whole increased compared with the 1992 survey, but the volume of their activities remains small, as indicated by the preponderant role of the state and the successors to the state enterprises in input supply.

Overall, half of farmers report that input prices are too high. This common complaint is particularly acute for farm machinery, spare parts, and fuel (Table 5.20). Yet a substantial proportion of farmers report that they do not experience any problems with supply of farm inputs and services. In 1994, as in 1992, private farmers did not report serious physical shortages of inputs and services. The proportion of farmers without supply problems

increased compared with the 1992 survey, while the proportion of farmers complaining of physical shortages (small to start with) decreased even further. Although farmers may not report problems with input supply, a high proportion apparently do not purchase fertilizers, chemicals, and veterinary drugs from any source (Table 5.19). The perception that prices are too high and difficulties financing purchase of farm inputs leads, according to the findings of this survey, to production technology using very low levels of purchased inputs.

Private farmers are evenly divided between those who feel that their access to supply channels is the same as the access of collective farms and those who believe they are more restricted in this respect (around 40% of respondents in each category).

Table 5.19. Use of Different Supply Channels for Farm Inputs and Services*

Input/Service	Collective farm	State sources#	Private sources	Farmers coop	Other	Private farmers acting as suppliers of farm inputs**
Seeds and seedlings	42	47	14	7	4	24
Feed	3	3	4	1	9	8
Young animals	6	16	15	1	6	5
Fertilizer	2	32	1	0	1	3
Herbicides/Pesticides	2	25	2	0	0	2
Purchase of machinery	27	71	6	5	2	33
Repairs and service	6	15	5	2	17	27
Spare parts	14	74	35	5	2	26
Fuel	4	89	14	2	1	31
Machinery services	14	8	22	17	11	54
Veterinary drugs	20	19	1	--	1	2
Veterinary services	30	12	4	0	1	2
Construction materials	7	47	8	1	2	3
Construction services	1	10	5	1	4	4
Consulting	13	28	17	21	3	34

*   Percent of 1030 respondents that report using the channels.
#   Includes the state-controlled consumer-cooperative network (*Tsentrosoyuz*).
**   Percent of respondents in each input/service category.

Table 5.20. Reported Difficulties with Purchase of Farm Inputs and Services (percent of respondents for each input/service)

Input/Service	Price too high	Not available	No problems	Input/Service	Price too high	Not available	No problems
Seeds and seedlings	60.1	2.5	37.3	Fuel	88.6	1.3	9.9
Feed	10.7	5.0	79.3	Machinery services	36.2	3.7	59.5
Young animals	19.7	4.2	71.2	Veterinary drugs	20.5	5.4	69.0
Fertilizer	82.1	2.1	15.5	Veterinary services	11.7	3.2	79.9
Herbicides/Pesticides	75.0	4.4	20.2	Construction materials	65.4	3.3	30.4
Purchase of machinery	91.2	1.4	7.2	Construction services	45.2	4.2	49.1
Repairs and service	50.6	3.1	45.5	Consulting	3.7	3.8	90.9
Spare parts	83.3	2.9	13.4	**Mean of responses**	**49.6**	**3.4**	**45.2**

Cooperation

Private farmers join with others for cooperative activities (Table 5.21). Three-quarters of private farmers report that they participate in the activity of farmers' organizations and cooperatives. AKKOR, the Russian national association of private farmers, has the highest participation rate (67%, similar to the participation rate in 1992). Over 70% participate in some form of joint activity in provision or use of farm services. The overall participation in joint activities is practically the same in the two surveys: 74% in 1994 compared to 78% in 1992. Novosibirsk and Rostov remain the provinces with the highest incidence of emergent cooperation among private farmers, as in the 1992 survey, while Pskov still has the least cooperation.

Between 30%-40% of respondents cooperate with other farmers in production, product marketing, input supply, use of machinery, or provision or receipt of credit. The participation rates in various activities reported in 1994 are on the whole identical to those in the 1992 survey (Table 5.21). Cooperative activity in processing increased in 1994 compared to 1992.

A number of farmers report owning a fraction of a machine (0.6 of a tractor or 0.3 of a truck). The frequency of such joint ownership in the sample is not very high, but it is not negligible (Table 5.22).

Table 5.21. Cooperation Among Private Farmers 1992-1994 (percent of respondents)

	1994	1992
Consulting	58.3	55.2
Marketing	32.5	33.0
Input supply	30.4	36.8
Machinery pool	42.5	35.2
Mutual credit	37.1	34.6
Joint production	26.6	31.0
Processing	7.9	0.8
Other	9.9	6.2

Table 5.22. Farmers Owning "Less than a Whole Machine"

Machine	Percent out of all farmers with machines in this category	Range of fractional ownership
Tractors	3.5	0.5-0.6
Trucks	4.5	0.3-0.5
Plows	4.0	0.3-0.8
Seeders	5.0	0.1-0.5
Harvesters	8.6	0.2-0.5
Grain combines	9.1	0.3-0.5
Other machinery	5.6	0.2-0.5

Debt and Finances

Three-quarters of the farmers in the sample are active in the credit markets, i.e., have outstanding debt or borrowed during 1993. Thus, 48% report that they have outstanding debt; 53% borrowed short-term (for durations of less than 6 months) in 1993; and 44% borrowed for durations longer than 6 months in 1993. Most of the borrowing, whether classified as short-term or long-term, appears to be for durations of less than one year: the level of outstanding debt is close to (and even somewhat lower than) the volume of borrowing reported for 1993. The average farm in the sample borrowed 3.3 million rubles in 1993, while the outstanding debt is 3.0 million rubles. This is understandable in an inflationary environment, where true long-term borrowing with maturities longer than one year is impossible without proper indexing mechanisms.

Comparison of borrowing and outstanding debt to the value of fixed assets reported by the farms in 1993 indicates that the level of debt was not large relative to reported value of assets. The median ratio of debt to assets and borrowing to assets over the farms in the sample was 0.12 and 0.14, respectively (median ratio is cited because the average ratio is distorted by extreme outliers).

Since debt is repaid from current cashflows, it is also relevant to examine the ratio of debt to sales (the so-called "credit-years" measure). In 1993, the average sales volume was 5.8 million rubles per farm, compared to around 3 million rubles borrowing or debt. The median ratio of outstanding debt to sales was 0.5 and the median ratio of borrowing to sales was 0.6, i.e., roughly six-months sales are required to repay the debt for 50% of the farms. For the upper quartile of the debt to sales distribution; i.e., for 25% of the farms with relatively high debt, about 14 months sales are required to repay outstanding debt. These data indicate that in 1993 most farms in the sample had sales revenue sufficient to cover their total outstanding debt, and were in this respect financially solvent. Since the debt is short term,

however, and since roll-over in Russia entails considerable uncertainty, service of this level of debt out of annual sales implies a squeeze on retained earnings of the farm operator and on the ability to finance investment out of equity.

Two-thirds of the farmers provide their creditors with collateral. Over 70% mortgage their machinery and equipment as collateral for credit. Another 25% use AKKOR guarantees to obtain credit. The house, the livestock, and the crops are not commonly used as collateral (they are used by fewer than 10% of respondents). Land is used as collateral only by 2% of respondents. These findings are similar to the 1992 survey, except that the role of AKKOR guarantees has declined significantly (Table 5.23).

Table 5.23. Collateral Used by Private Farmers: 1992-1994 (percent of farmers using collateral)

	1994	1992
Machinery and equipment	73	51
House	6	5
Livestock	12	4
Crops	5	3
Land	2	6
AKKOR guarantees	27	57
Percent of all respondents who use collateral	64	67

Farmers typically report that interest rates are prohibitively high, yet most borrowed in 1993 at highly preferential rates. Nearly 70% of farmers borrowed at annual rates below 30%, mostly at 28%, although 10% of farmers reported that they took loans for more than 6 months at 8% annually. This low interest rates represent centrally allocated credits. The average borrowing rate is not much different for short- and medium-term loans (resp. 60% and 69%). However, the difference is statistically significant, and a somewhat higher percentage of medium-term borrowing is done at rates in excess of 200% per annum. Truncating the observations with reported interest rate below 30%, we obtain for farmers an average rate of 132% for short-term borrowing and 155% for medium-term borrowing, which is very close to the interest rates reported by farm-enterprise managers (155% short-term and 171% long-term).

Three-quarters of the farmers report that they cannot borrow all that they need because the interest rate is high. A similar percentage of respondents report that they have difficulties getting credit (both short- and medium-term). The bank is the main source of credit for private farmers (67% long-term credit for investment and 50% short-term credit for current expenses). One-quarter of the farmers rely on relatives to advance money for current expenses in case of need. Fully 20% of farmers report that they have no source to borrow either short- or long-term. The credit link to the collective farm enterprise has been effectively eliminated: none of the respondents indicate that they can borrow from the farm enterprise.

Despite the pronounced commercial orientation of private farmers, 60% of the sampled farms do not report any accounts receivable. This probably highlights the predominance of cash sales on local markets and to private individuals. For 40% of farmers in the sample who carry accounts receivable, state procurement organizations are responsible for three-quarters of the total. The remaining 25% of debtors are represented in roughly equal proportions by commercial trade organizations, other enterprises (collective farms and processors), private farmers and other individuals, and local government.

The average amount of accounts receivable per farm matches the reported value of working capital (both are around 2.8 million rubles in 1994). This means that private farms practically do not carry inventories. More importantly, the accounts receivable virtually balance the outstanding debt or the current borrowing of the average farm (around 3 million rubles), so that the net indebtedness of private farms is virtually zero. Based on 1993

average sales of 5.8 million rubles, accounts receivable of 2.8 million rubles represent nearly six months of sales, which for a small farmer is a long time to wait for money in an inflationary environment. The farmers' arrears compare unfavorably with those of farm enterprises, which collect their sales income in about four months.

Table 5.24. Growth of Assets and Sales in Private Farms (thousand rubles)

	Per farm average	
	Assets	*Sales*
1990	32	15
1991	941	109
1992	3150	1418
1993	31572	5815
Change 90-93	**× 987**	**× 388**
Price index change*	× 481	× 125

* Change of industrial prices for assets and change of agricultural prices for sales.

The average farm in the sample increased the nominal value of its assets by a factor of nearly 1000 between 1990 and 1993 (Table 5.24). The sales revenue in the same period increased only by a factor of 400. The differential increase in values of assets and sales reflects the deterioration of agricultural prices relative to industrial prices over the period. The value of assets roughly doubled when deflated by an index of industrial prices. The value of sales per farm roughly tripled when deflated by an index of agricultural prices. The volume of production and sales on the private farms thus increased substantially, although not enough to compensate for the deterioration in agricultural prices relative to industrial prices, nor for the galloping increase in consumer prices (which rose by a factor of 640 between 1990-1993).

Table 5.25. Sources of Annual Investment Flows (in percent)

	1990	1991	1992	1993
Own savings	44.6	8.2	10.3	15.1
Asset share	1.4	4.0	1.8	10.9
Bank loans	46.8	85.3	76.6	40.4
Loans from relatives	7.2	1.1	1.4	0.8
Loans from enterprise	0.0	0.3	0.8	0.1
Government grants	0.0	0.5	0.3	0.3
From Russian farmers' fund	0.0	0.0	0.0	0.0
Other sources	0.0	0.5	8.7	32.2
Number of responding farms	*15*	*113*	*617*	*973*

Table 5.26. Cost-to-Sales Ratio in Russian Farms: 1990-1993
(ratio less than 1 implies excess of sales revenue over production costs)

	Average ratio*	Median ratio	Upper quartile	Percent of unprofitable farms	Number of respondents out of 1030
1990	1.74	1.50	2.00	67	9
1991	0.86	1.17	1.97	58	46
1992	0.75	0.84	1.43	36	399
1993	0.67	0.76	1.00	25	911

*Ratio of average costs to average sales for matched farms in each year.

Since 1991 private farms have been financed largely with outside money rather than savings or retained earnings of the operator. The proportion of equity in annual investment has been 10%-15% since 1991. Only in 1990 did farms finance fully half of the total annual investment from own savings (Fig. 5.6). Bank credits provide most of the financing for investment since 1991. Government grants, money from the Russian farmers' fund, and money from the farm enterprise are reported to be negligible over all years (Table 5.25).

The asset share received by former employees on exit from the large-scale farm enterprise is basically intended to provide the startup capital for new private farms. Yet the asset share constitutes but a small part of the annual investment in the farm (Table 5.25). Since half the former employees report that on leaving the enterprise they received

an allocation of assets in kind and another 20% received the value of their asset share in cash, the small weight of the asset share in total farm investment is not a reflection of reluctance or

Fig. 5.6. Sources of Investment Funds

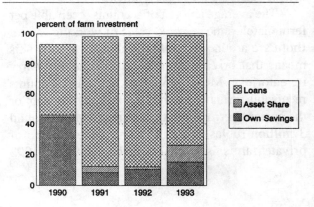

percent of farm investment

tardiness on behalf of farm-enterprise managers in allocating and distributing assets to new farmers. This is rather a result of the inherently low value of asset shares relative to the required investment in a new farm. Thus, as reported by managers of farm enterprises (see Chapter 3), the average asset share in 1992 was valued at around 70,000 rubles, which is 2% of the total assets of an average private farm as given in Table 5.24; in 1993, the average asset share was valued at 2.2 million rubles, which represents less than 7% of total farm assets shown in Table 5.24.

Sales revenues on the whole exceeded production costs in 1992 and 1993 (Table 5.26). The proportion of loss-making farms decreased over time, and in 1993 only 25% of the responding farms reported costs higher than revenues.

Profitability appears to improve with the age of the farm: in 1993, the percentage of unprofitable farms among those registered in 1990-1992 was below the average (17%), while fully 36% of farms registered in 1993 are reported to earn losses. Actual profitability, however, may be lower than perceived profitability, since proper adjustment for inflation may turn accounting profit into a loss. Yet in general, the picture that emerges from the survey does not support the conventional view of private farms that groan under a crushing burden of debt and suffer continual losses. Although some private farms failed financially and ceased operations, the survey indicates that in early 1994 private farmers were a small but significant and persistent component of the Russian farm structure.

World Bank Publications

Prices and credit terms vary from country to country. Consult your local distributor before placing an order.

ALBANIA
Adrion Ltd.
Perlat Rexhepi Str.
Pall. 9, Shk. 1, Ap. 4
Tirana
Tel: (1) 815-8156
Fax: (1) 815-8354

ARGENTINA
Oficina del Libro Internacional
Av. Cordoba 1877
1120 Buenos Aires
Tel: (1) 815-8156
Fax: (1) 815-8354

AUSTRALIA, FIJI, PAPUA NEW GUINEA, SOLOMON ISLANDS, VANUATU, AND WESTERN SAMOA
D.A. Information Services
648 Whitehorse Road
Mitcham 3132
Victoria
Tel: (61) 3 9210 7777
Fax: (61) 3 9210 7788
URL: http://www.dadirect.com.au

AUSTRIA
Gerold and Co.
Graben 31
A-1011 Wien
Tel: (1) 533-50-14-0
Fax: (1) 512-47-31-29

BANGLADESH
Micro Industries Development
Assistance Society (MIDAS)
House 5, Road 16
Dhanmondi R/Area
Dhaka 1209
Tel: (2) 326427
Fax: (2) 811188

BELGIUM
Jean De Lannoy
Av. du Roi 202
1060 Brussels
Tel: (2) 538-5169
Fax: (2) 538-0841

BRAZIL
Publicações Tecnicas Internacionais Ltda.
Rua Peixoto Gomide, 209
01409 Sao Paulo, SP.
Tel: (11) 259-6644
Fax: (11) 258-6990

CANADA
Renouf Publishing Co. Ltd.
1294 Algoma Road
Ottawa, Ontario K1B 3W8
Tel: 613-741-4333
Fax: 613-741-5439

8, Da Fo Si Dong Jie
Beijing
Tel: (1) 333-8257
Fax: (1) 401-7365

COLOMBIA
Infoenlace Ltda.
Apartado Aereo 34270
Bogotá D.E.
Tel: (1) 285-2798
Fax: (1) 285-2798

COTE D'IVOIRE
Centre d'Edition et de Diffusion
Africaines (CEDA)
04 B.P. 541
Abidjan 04 Plateau
Tel: 225-24-6510
Fax: 225-25-0567

CYPRUS
Center of Applied Research
Cyprus College
6, Diogenes Street, Engomi
P.O. Box 2006
Nicosia
Tel: 244-1730
Fax: 246-2051

CZECH REPUBLIC
National Information Center
prodejna, Konviktska 5
CS - 113 57 Prague 1
Tel: (2) 2422-9433
Fax: (2) 2422-1484
URL: http://www.nis.cz/

DENMARK
SamfundsLitteratur
Rosenoerns Allé 11
DK-1970 Frederiksberg C
Tel: (31)-351942
Fax: (31)-357822

ECUADOR
Facultad Latinoamericana de
Ciencias Sociales
FLACSO-SEDE Ecuador
Calle Ulpiano Paez 118
y Av. Patria
Quito, Ecuador
Tel: (2) 542 714; 542 716; 528 200
Fax: (2) 566 139

EGYPT, ARAB REPUBLIC OF
Al Ahram
Al Galaa Street
Cairo
Tel: (2) 578-6083
Fax: (2) 578-6833

The Middle East Observer
41, Sherif Street
Cairo
Tel: (2) 393-9732
Fax: (2) 393-9732

FINLAND
Akateeminen Kirjakauppa
P.O. Box 23
FIN-00371 Helsinki
Tel: (0) 12141
Fax: (0) 121-4441
URL: http://booknet.cultnet.fi/aka/

75116 Paris
Tel: (1) 40-69-30-56/57
Fax: (1) 40-69-30-68

GERMANY
UNO-Verlag
Poppelsdorfer Allee 55
53115 Bonn
Tel: (228) 212940
Fax: (228) 217492

GREECE
Papasotiriou S.A.
35, Stournara Str.
106 82 Athens
Tel: (1) 364-1826
Fax: (1) 364-8254

HONG KONG, MACAO
Asia 2000 Ltd.
Sales & Circulation Department
Seabird House, unit 1101-02
22-28 Wyndham Street, Central
Hong Kong
Tel: 852 2530-1409
Fax: 852 2526-1107
URL: http://www.sales@asia2000.com.hk

HUNGARY
Foundation for Market
Economy
Dombovari Ut 17-19
H-1117 Budapest
Tel: 36 1 204 2951 or
36 1 204 2948
Fax: 36 1 204 2953

INDIA
Allied Publishers Ltd.
751 Mount Road
Madras - 600 002
Tel: (44) 852-3938
Fax: (44) 852-0649

INDONESIA
Pt. Indira Limited
Jalan Borobudur 20
P.O. Box 181
Jakarta 10320
Tel: (21) 390-4290
Fax: (21) 421-4289

IRAN
Kowkab Publishers
P.O. Box 19575-511
Tehran
Tel: (21) 258-3723
Fax: 98 (21) 258-3723

Ketab Sara Co. Publishers
Khaled Eslamboli Ave.,
6th Street
Kusheh Delafrooz No. 8
Tehran
Tel: 8717819 or 8716104
Fax: 8862479

IRELAND
Government Supplies Agency
Oifig an tSoláthair
4-5 Harcourt Road
Dublin 2
Tel: (1) 461-3111
Fax: (1) 475-2670

Tel Aviv 61560
Tel: (3) 5285-397
Fax: (3) 5285-397

R.O.Y. International
PO Box 13056
Tel Aviv 61130
Tel: (3) 5461423
Fax: (3) 5461442

Palestinian Authority/Middle East
Index Information Services
P.O.B. 19502 Jerusalem
Tel: (2) 271219

ITALY
Licosa Commissionaria Sansoni SPA
Via Duca Di Calabria, 1/1
Casella Postale 552
50125 Firenze
Tel: (55) 645-415
Fax: (55) 641-257

JAMAICA
Ian Randle Publishers Ltd.
206 Old Hope Road
Kingston 6
Tel: 809-927-2085
Fax: 809-977-0243

JAPAN
Eastern Book Service
Hongo 3-Chome,
Bunkyo-ku 113
Tokyo
Tel: (03) 3818-0861
Fax: (03) 3818-0864
URL: http://www.bekkoame.or.jp/~svt-ebs

KENYA
Africa Book Service (E.A.) Ltd.
Quaran House, Mfangano Street
P.O. Box 45245
Nairobi
Tel: (2) 23641
Fax: (2) 330272

KOREA, REPUBLIC OF
Daejon Trading Co. Ltd.
P.O. Box 34
Yeoeida
Seoul
Tel: (2) 785-1631/4
Fax: (2) 784-0315

MALAYSIA
University of Malaya Cooperative
Bookshop, Limited
P.O. Box 1127
Jalan Pantai Baru
59700 Kuala Lumpur
Tel: (3) 756-5000
Fax: (3) 755-4424

MEXICO
INFOTEC
Apartado Postal 22-860
14060 Tlalpan,
Mexico D.F.
Tel: (5) 606-0011
Fax: (5) 606-0386

NETHERLANDS
De Lindeboom/InOr-Publikaties
P.O. Box 202
7480 AE Haaksbergen
Tel: (53) 574-0004
Fax: (53) 572-9296

Moscow 101831
Tel: (95) 917 87 49
Fax: (95) 917 92 59

SAUDI ARABIA, QATAR
Jarir Book Store
P.O. Box 3196
Riyadh 11471
Tel: (1) 477-3140
Fax: (1) 477-2940

SINGAPORE, TAIWAN, MYANMAR, BRUNEI
Asahgate Publishing Asia
Pacific Pte. Ltd.
41 Kallang Pudding Road #04-03
Golden Wheel Building
Singapore 349316
Tel: (65) 741-5166
Fax: (65) 742-9356
e-mail: ashgate@asianconnect.com

SLOVAK REPUBLIC
Slovart G.T.G. Ltd.
Krupinska 4
P.O. Box 152
852 99 Bratislava 5
Tel: (7) 839472
Fax: (7) 839485

SOUTH AFRICA, BOTSWANA
For single titles:
Oxford University Press
Southern Africa
P.O. Box 1141
Cape Town 8000
Tel: (21) 45-7266
Fax: (21) 45-7265

For subscription orders:
International Subscription Service
P.O. Box 41095
Craighall
Johannesburg 2024
Tel: (11) 880-1448
Fax: (11) 880-6248

SPAIN
Mundi-Prensa Libros, S.A.
Castello 37
28001 Madrid
Tel: (1) 431-3399
Fax: (1) 575-3998
http://www.tsai.es/mprensa

Mundi-Prensa Barcelona
Consell de Cent, 391
08009 Barcelona
Tel: (3) 488-3009
Fax: (3) 487-7659

SRI LANKA, THE MALDIVES
Lake House Bookshop
P.O. Box 244
100, Sir Chittampalam A.
Gardiner Mawatha
Colombo 2
Tel: (1) 32105
Fax: (1) 432104

SWEDEN
Fritzes Customer Service
Regeringsgaton 12
S-106 47 Stockholm
Tel: (8) 690 90 90
Fax: (8) 21 47 77

Tel: (8) 705-97-50
Fax: (8) 27-00-71

SWITZERLAND
Librairie Payot
Service Institutionnel
Côtes-de-Montbenon 30
1002 Lausanne
Tel: (021)-320-2511
Fax: (021)-311-1393

Van Diermen Editions Techniq
Ch. de Lacuez 41
CH1807 Blonay
Tel: (021) 943 2673
Fax: (021) 943 3605

TANZANIA
Oxford University Press
Maktaba Street
PO Box 5299
Dar es Salaam
Tel: (51) 29209
Fax: (51) 46822

THAILAND
Central Books Distribution
306 Silom Road
Bangkok
Tel: (2) 235-5400
Fax: (2) 237-8321

TRINIDAD & TOBAGO, JAM.
Systematics Studies Unit
#9 Watts Street
Curepe
Trinidad, West Indies
Tel: 809-662-5654
Fax: 809-662-5654

UGANDA
Gustro Ltd.
Madhvani Building
PO Box 9997
Plot 16/4 Jinja Rd.
Kampala
Tel/Fax: (41) 254763

UNITED KINGDOM
Microinfo Ltd.
P.O. Box 3
Alton, Hampshire GU34 2PG
England
Tel: (1420) 86848
Fax: (1420) 89889

ZAMBIA
University Bookshop
Great East Road Campus
Lusaka
Tel: (1) 213221 Ext. 482

ZIMBABWE
Longman Zimbabwe (Pte.)Ltd.
Tourle Road, Ardbennie
P.O. Box ST125
Southerton
Harare
Tel: (4) 662711
Fax: (4) 662716

NIGERIA
University Press Limited
Three Crowns Building Jericho
Private Mail Bag 5095
Ibadan
Tel: (22) 41-1356
Fax: (22) 41-2056

NORWAY
Narvesen Information Center
Book Department
P.O.B. 6125 Etterstad
N-0602 Oslo 6
Tel: (22) 57-3300
Fax: (22) 68-1901

PAKISTAN
Mirza Book Agency
65, Shahrah-e-Quaid-e-Azam
Lahore 54000
Tel: (42) 7353601
Fax: (42) 7585283

Oxford University Press
5 Bangalore Town
Sharae Faisal
PO Box 13033
Karachi-75350
Tel: (21) 446307
Fax: (21) 454-7640

PERU
Editorial Desarrollo SA
Apartado 3824
Lima 1
Tel: (14) 285380
Fax: (14) 286628

PHILIPPINES
International Booksource Center Inc.
Suite 720, Cityland 10
Condominium Tower 2
H.V dela Costa, corner
Valero St.
Makati, Metro Manila
Tel: (2) 817-9676
Fax: (2) 817-1741

POLAND
International Publishing Service
Ul. Piekna 31/37
00-577 Warzawa
Tel: (2) 628-6089
Fax: (2) 621-7255

PORTUGAL
Livraria Portugal
Rua Do Carmo 70-74
1200 Lisbon
Tel: (1) 347-4982
Fax: (1) 347-0264

ROMANIA
Compani De Librarii Bucuresti S.A.
Str. Lipscani no. 26, sector 3
Bucharest
Tel: (1) 613 9645
Fax: (1) 312 4000

Tel: (9) 524-8119
Fax: (9) 524-8067

Recent World Bank Discussion Papers *(continued)*

No. 291   *Transforming Payment Systems: Meeting the Needs of Emerging Market Economies.* Setsuya Sato and David Burras Humphrey

No. 292   *Regulated Deregulation of the Financial System in Korea.* Ismail Dalla and Deena Khatkhate

No. 293   *Design Issues in Rural Finance.* Orlando J. Sacay and Bikki K. Randhawa

No. 294   *Financing Health Services Through User Fees and Insurance: Case Studies from Sub-Saharan Africa.* R. Paul Shaw and Martha Ainsworth

No. 295   *The Participation of Nongovernmental Organizations in Poverty Alleviation: The Case Study of the Honduras Social Investment Fund Project.* Anna Kathryn Vandever Webb, Kye Woo Lee, and Anna Maria Sant'Anna

No. 296   *Reforming the Energy Sector in Transition Economies: Selected Experience and Lessons.* Dale Gray

No. 297   *Assessing Sector Institutions: Lessons of Experience from Zambia's Education Sector.* Rogerio F. Pinto and Angelous J. Mrope

No. 298   *Uganda's AIDS Crisis: Its Implications for Development.* Jill Armstrong

No. 299   *Towards a Payments System Law for Developing and Transition Economies.* Raj Bhala

No. 300   *Africa Can Compete! Export Opportunities and Challenges in Garments and Home Products in the European Market.* Tyler Biggs, Margaret Miller, Caroline Otto, and Gerald Tyler

No. 301   *Review and Outlook for the World Oil Market.* Shane S. Streifel

No. 302   *The Broad Sector Approach to Investment Lending: Sector Investment Programs.* Peter Harrold and Associates

No. 303   *Institutional Adjustment and Adjusting to Institutions.* Robert Klitgaard

No. 304   *Putting Institutional Economics to Work: From Participation to Governance.* Robert Picciotto

No. 305   *Pakistan's Public Agricultural Enterprises: Inefficiencies, Market Distortions, and Proposals for Reform.* Rashid Faruqee, Ridwan Ali, and Yusuf Choudhry

No. 306   *Grameen Bank: Performance and Stability.* Shahidur R. Khandker, Baqui Khalily, and Zahed Khan

No. 307   *The Uruguay Round and the Developing Economies.* Edited by Will Martin and L. Alan Winters

No. 308   *Bank Governance Contracts: Establishing Goals and Accountability in Bank Restructuring.* Richard P. Roulier

No. 309   *Public and Private Secondary Education in Developing Countries: A Comparative Study.* Emmanuel Jimenez and Marlaine E. Lockheed with contributions by Donald Cox, Eduardo Luna, Vicente Paqueo, M. L. de Vera, and Nongnuch Wattanawaha

No. 310   *Practical Lessons for Africa from East Asia in Industrial and Trade Policies.* Peter Harrold, Malathi Jayawickrama, and Deepak Bhattasali

No. 311   *The Impact of the Uruguay Round on Africa.* Peter Harrold

No. 312   *Procurement and Disbursement Manual for Projects with Community Participation.* Gita Gopal

No. 313   *Harnessing Information for Development: A Proposal for a World Bank Group Strategy.* Eduardo Talero and Philip Gaudette

No. 314   *Colombia's Pension Reform: Fiscal and Macroeconomic Effects.* Klaus Schmidt-Hebbel

No. 315   *Land Quality Indicators.* Christian Pieri, Julian Dumanski, Ann Hamblin, and Anthony Young

No. 316   *Sustainability of a Government Targeted Credit Program: Evidence from Bangladesh.* Shahidur R. Khandker, Zahed Khan, and Baqui Khalily

No. 317   *Selected Social Safety Net Programs in the Philippines: Targeting, Cost-Effectiveness, and Options for Reform.* Kalanidhi Subbarao, Akhter U. Ahmed, and Tesfaye Teklu

No. 318   *Private Sector Development During Transition: The Visegrad Countries.* Michael S. Borish and Michel Noël

No. 319   *Education Achievements and School Efficiency in Rural Bangladesh.* Shahidur R. Khandker

No. 320   *Household and Intrahousehold Impacts of the Grameen Bank and Similar Targeted Credit Programs in Bangladesh.* Mark M. Pitt and Shahidur R. Khandker

No. 321   *Clearance and Settlement Systems for Securities: Critical Design Choices in Emerging Market Economies.* Jeff Stehm.

No. 322   *Selecting Development Projects for the World Bank.* Jean Baneth

No. 323   *Evaluating Public Spending: A Framework for Public Expenditure Reviews.* Sanjay Pradhan

No. 324   *Credit Programs in Bangladesh: Performance and Sustainability.* Shahidur R. Khandker and Baqui Khalily

No. 325   *Institutional and Entrepreneurial Leadership in the Brazilian Science and Technology Sector:Setting a New Agenda.* Edited by Lauritz Holm-Nielsen, Michael Crawford, and Alcyone Saliba

No. 326   *The East Asian Miracle and Information Technology: Strategic Management of Technological Learning.* Nagy Hanna, Sandor Boyson, and Shakuntala Gunaratne

THE WORLD BANK

A partner in strengthening economies
and expanding markets
to improve the quality of life
for people everywhere,
especially the poorest

Headquarters
1818 H Street, N.W.
Washington, D.C. 20433, U.S.A.

Telephone: (202) 477-1234
Facsimile: (202) 477-6391
Telex: MCI 64145 WORLDBANK
           MCI 248423 WORLDBANK
Cable Address: INTBAFRAD
                 WASHINGTONDC
World Wide Web: http://www.worldbank.org
E-mail: books@worldbank.org

European Office
66, avenue d'Iéna
75116 Paris, France

Telephone: (1) 40.69.30.00
Facsimile: (1) 40.69.30.66
Telex: 640651

Tokyo Office
Kokusai Building
1-1 Marunouchi 3-chome
Chiyoda-ku, Tokyo 100, Japan

Telephone: (3) 3214-5001
Facsimile: (3) 3214-3657
Telex: 26838

ISBN 0-8213-3655-X